Essential Grammar in Use Supplementary Exercises

WITH ANSWERS

Helen Naylor
with **Raymond Murphy**

CAMBRIDGE
UNIVERSITY PRESS

PUBLISHED BY THE PRESS SYNDICATE OF THE UNIVERSITY OF CAMBRIDGE
The Pitt Building, Trumpington Street, Cambridge, United Kingdom

CAMBRIDGE UNIVERSITY PRESS
The Edinburgh Building, Cambridge CB2 2RU, UK
40 West 20th Street, New York, NY 10011–4211, USA
10 Stamford Road, Oakleigh, VIC 3166, Australia
Ruiz de Alarcón 13, 28014 Madrid, Spain
Dock House, The Waterfront, Cape Town 8001, South Africa

http://www.cambridge.org

© Cambridge University Press 1996

First published 1996
2nd reprint 2001

Printed in the United Kingdom at the University Press, Cambridge

A catalogue record for this book is available from the British Library

ISBN 0 521 46997 X Supplementary Exercises (with answers)
ISBN 0 521 46998 8 Supplementary Exercises (without answers)
ISBN 0 521 55928 6 Essential Grammar in Use (with answers)
ISBN 0 521 55927 8 Essential Grammar in Use (without answers)

Contents

Key

To the student

This book is for elementary (and lower intermediate) students who want extra practice in grammar. It covers most of the grammar areas in *Essential Grammar in Use*. You can use it without a teacher.

The book has 184 exercises. Each exercise relates to a particular part of *Essential Grammar in Use*. You can find the *Essential Grammar in Use* unit number in the top right-hand corner of each page. You can use this book if you don't have *Essential Grammar in Use* because all the answers, with lots of alternatives, are given in the Key (pages 95–106). But if you want an explanation of the grammar points, you'll need to check in *Essential Grammar in Use*.

The grammar points covered in this book are not in order of difficulty, so you can go straight to the parts where you need most practice. But where there are several exercises on one grammar point, you will find that the easier ones come first. So it is a good idea to follow the exercise order in that section.

Many of the exercises are in the form of letters, conversations or short articles. You can use these as models for writing or speaking practice.

To the teacher

Essential Grammar in Use Supplementary Exercises offers extra practice of most of the grammar covered in *Essential Grammar in Use*. Much of the language is contextualised within dialogues, letters, articles, etc., encouraging students to consider meaning as well as form. The book can be used as self-study material or as a basis for further practice in class or as homework.
It is designed for students who have already worked through the exercises in *Essential Grammar in Use* (or elsewhere), but who need more, or more challenging, practice. It is particularly useful for revision work.

The exercises are organised in the same order as the units of *Essential Grammar in Use*, and the numbers of the relevant *Essential Grammar in Use* units are shown in the top right-hand corner of each page. Although the grammar areas are not covered in order of difficulty in the book as a whole, there is a progression where several exercises are offered on one area. For example, Exercise 7 requires students to use given verbs in the correct form, Exercise 8 requires them to write complete positive and negative sentences and Exercise 9 requires them to write complete questions within the context of a conversation. The contextualised practice in the book offers the opportunity for much further practice, using the exercises as models or springboards for speaking and writing practice of a freer nature. The symbol ☺ is used where a student is required to write freely from personal experience.

Thanks

For trying out exercises, and offering valuable comments: The English Department, Al Azhar University, Cairo, Egypt; The British Council, Athens, Greece; International House, Lódź, Poland; The British Council, Bologna, Italy; Instituto Español de Bachillerato, Aixovall, Andorra; Gabriela Brunner, Fernando García Clemente, Cemile Iskenderoğlu, Dr Felicity O'Dell, Lelio Pallini, Dr Ramzy Radwan.

I would also like to thank Nóirín Burke and Jeanne McCarten at Cambridge University Press for their help and support. Illustrated by Amanda MacPhail, Mark Peppé and Bill Piggins. Layout by Newton Harris. Edited by Geraldine Mark.

am/is/are

1 Complete the sentences. Use the words in the box.

am ('m)	is ('s)	are ('re)
am not ('m not)	is not (isn't)	are not (aren't)

1 David's new bicycle ...*is*... blue.
2 A: Are these your books?
   B: No, they *aren't.*
3 My children ...*are*... 8 and 6 years old.
4 I *'m not.* interested in baseball. I think it's boring.
5 We can walk to the supermarket. It *isn't* far.
6 A: Are you a teacher?
   B: Yes, I ...*am*...
7 A: ...*Are*... those birds from South America?
   B: The red one ...*IS*..., but the blue one ...*Isn't*...
8 When ...*is*... your birthday?
9 Kate and Sandra *aren't* at work today because it is a holiday.
10 You ...*are*... wrong. 9 x 9 is 81, not 82.
11 ...*Is*... this is the right bus for the city centre?
12 A: Where ...*are*... my shoes?
   B: In your bedroom.

2 Complete the sentences. Use one of the question forms in the box + **is** or **are**.

Where	Who	What
How	Why	How much
What colour	How old	

1 A: *Where are* my keys?   B: On the table.
2 A: *What's* the time, please?   B: Half past five.
3 A: *How's* your headache now?   B: Much better, thank you.
4 A: *Where 're* the holiday photographs?   B: In your handbag.
5 A: *How old IS* that clock?   B: Three hundred years old.
6 A: *What colour are* your new shoes?   B: Red.
7 A: *Why's* Simon happy today?   B: Because it's his birthday.
8 A: *Where's* Maria from?   B: Spain, I think.
9 A: *How much are* these trousers?   B: They're £40.
10 A: *Who's* that man in the car?   B: My uncle.
11 A: *Why 're* the banks closed today?   B: Because it's a holiday.

3 Write positive or negative sentences. Begin in Box A and choose an ending from Box B.

A		B
1 ~~Peter's parents~~		at work this week. I'm on holiday.
2 The Andes		the capital of the USA.
3 New York		a hot country.
4 Football	+ am/am not +	good for you.
5 Paul	is/isn't	very high mountains.
6 Britain	are/aren't	British. She's American.
7 All the shops		~~on holiday.~~
8 I		closed at lunchtime.
9 Too many chocolates		21 years old today.
10 Sally's teacher		a popular sport in Britain.

1 Peter's parents are on holiday.
2 The Andes ....
3 New York ....
4 ....
5 ....
6 ....
7 ....
8 ....
9 ....
10 ....

4 Look at the picture of a family group, and ask questions about the people. Read the answers to the questions first.

YOU: (1) Who's that man?
MARIA: That's my father. He's a dentist.
YOU: (2) How old is he ?
MARIA: He's 45.
YOU: (3) Is that your mother?
MARIA: Yes, it is. She's a dentist, too.
YOU: (4) Who's that girl ?
MARIA: That's my sister, Laura.
YOU: (5) How old is she ?
MARIA: She's 23.
YOU: (6) Is that your brother?
MARIA: No, it's Laura's husband.
YOU: (7) What is his name
MARIA: Ferdinand.
YOU: (8) Are those your grandparents?
MARIA: Yes, they are. That's my mother's father and my father's mother!

YOU   MARIA

28/4

5 Use the words in the box below to write sentences. Some of your sentences must be questions (**Where is …?**, **Are your parents …?**, etc.). Use each word at least once.

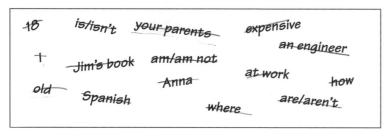

~~18~~	is/isn't	~~your parents~~	expensive
			~~an engineer~~
~~+~~	~~Jim's book~~	~~am/am not~~	
			~~at work~~	~~how~~
~~old~~	~~Anna~~		
	~~Spanish~~	~~where~~	~~are/aren't~~

1 Anna isn't Spanish.
2 Where is Jim's book?
3 Are your parents old?
4 I am not an engineer.
5 Jim's book is not expensive.
6 How old is Anna?
7 Are your parents at work?
8 Is your sister 18?
9 _____
10 _____

I am doing (present continuous)

6 How do you spell it? Write these verbs in the continuous form (**-ing**) in the correct list.

~~help~~	~~put~~	~~decide~~	~~die~~	~~swim~~	listen	~~have~~	~~forget~~	write
~~arrive~~	~~play~~	~~begin~~	~~start~~	~~come~~	stop	~~win~~	~~work~~	~~laugh~~
~~live~~	~~lie~~	~~wear~~	~~tie~~	~~cry~~	~~dance~~	~~dig~~	~~make~~	~~rob~~

+ -ing	t → tt, p → pp, *etc.*	e → ing	ie → ying
helping	putting	deciding	dying
playing	swimming	dancing	tying
wearing	stopping	coming	lying
crying	winning	writing	
listening	robbing	trying	
working	beginning	making	
starting	digging	having	
laughing	forgetting	arriving	

3

28/4

7 Complete the text about Jane and Mary who are in their office. Use the present continuous (**is/are** + **-ing**) of the verbs in the box. Sometimes the verb is negative (**isn't/aren't** + **-ing**).

| ~~write~~ | ~~drink~~ | ~~read~~ | ~~work~~ | ~~ring~~ | listen | ~~have~~ |
| ~~think~~ | make | ~~sing~~ | ask | ~~talk~~ | ~~stand~~ | sit |

10.30 a.m. Jane is in her office. She (1) _is reading_ some letters and (2) _writing_ her replies. Her secretary, Mary, (3) _is making_ some coffee. She (4) _is singing_ a song.

10.40 a.m. Jane and Mary (5) _are drinking_ their coffee. Jane (6) _is thinking_ about her holiday plans, but Mary (7) _is talking_ to her. She (8) _is talking_ about her new car. They (9) _aren't working_ at the moment; they (10) _are having_ their coffee break.

10.50 a.m. The telephone (11) _is ringing_ and that is the end of their break. Now it's back to work.

10.55 a.m. Jane (12) _is standing_ at her desk. She (13) _is standing_ next to the window and (14) _asking_ some questions to an important customer.

8 Look at the picture and the description. Re-write the description to make it correct.

Steve is reading a newspaper. The children, Sam and Eric, are playing with a ball. They are both wearing sunglasses. Pam is cooking chicken. She's laughing because the smoke is getting in her eyes. Jo is standing with her mother and is listening to music on her personal stereo. She is eating an orange. Fred, the dog, is lying on the grass asleep.

1 Steve _isn't reading the newspaper. He's reading a book._
2 Sam and Eric _aren't playing with a ball. They are playing with a train._
3 _Eric isn't wearing glasses. He is wearing a hat._
4 _Pam isn't cooking chicken. She is cooking fish._
5 _Pam isn't laughing. She's crying._
6 _Jo isn't standing with her mother. She is lying on the grass._
7 _She isn't eating an orange. She is eating a banana._
8 _Fred isn't lying. It's playing with a ball._

9 You can hear your mother talking to your grandfather on the telephone. Write the questions your *29/4* grandfather is asking, using the present continuous (**is/are** + **-ing**). Look at all the answers first.

GRANDFATHER: (1) ....*Are*.... the children ...*watching TV?*........

MOTHER: No, they're in bed.

GRANDFATHER: (2) ...*Are they*.................................... reading?

MOTHER: No, they aren't. They're asleep.

GRANDFATHER: (3) ...*What's*.... Simon ...*doing*............?

MOTHER: He's writing a postcard and watching TV at the same time.

GRANDFATHER: (4) ...*What is he watching*..............?

MOTHER: A travel programme about India.

GRANDFATHER: (5) ...*Is*.......... Anna ...*watching TV*.... ?

MOTHER: No, she isn't watching it. She's in the kitchen, cooking the dinner.

GRANDFATHER: (6) ...*What are you doing*............?

MOTHER: Lying on the floor and talking to you!

I do/work/like etc. (present simple)   **Units 5–7**

10 Which of the underlined verbs is right? The information is about the USA.

1 Most shops usually open/~~opens~~ at 8.30 a.m. and close/~~closes~~ at 6.00 p.m.
2 The banks ~~doesn't~~/don't usually close at lunchtime.
3 Many children ~~has~~/have a computer at home.
4 The New York subway usually works/~~work~~ very well.
5 It doesn't/~~don't~~ often snow in California.
6 Most people don't/~~doesn't~~ work on Sundays.
7 The capital city, Washington, ~~have~~/has a population of about one million.
8 Many people in Los Angeles speak/~~speaks~~ Spanish.
9 Schoolchildren don't/~~doesn't~~ usually wear uniform.

11 Complete the sentences using the verbs below each picture. Put the verbs into the present simple. For the last sentence for each picture put the verb into the negative.

1 **A lion**

run/eat/have/sleep

It *has* a tail.
It *runs* very fast.
It *sleeps* a lot.
It *doesn't eat* fish.

2 **Marc, aged 6 months**

read/cry/live/drink

He *lives* with his Mum and Dad.
He *drinks* orange juice.
He *cries* a lot.
He *doesn't read* books.

3 **The Sahara Desert**

shine/rain/fall/live

The sun *shines* every day.
Not many people *live* there.
The temperature *falls* at night.
It *doesn't rain* very much.

4 **Birds**

eat/have/like/fly

They *have* wings.
They *eat* insects.
They *fly* long distances.
They *don't like* cats.

Ben does.

12 Ten sentences are wrong and two sentences are right. Correct the mistakes where necessary.

1 David never take the bus to work. *David never takes the bus to work.*
2 Go you to the office every day? *Do you go to the office every day?*
3 My car don't work when it is cold. *My car doesn't work when it is cold.*
4 What time the film starts? *What time does the film start?*
5 Ben's sister don't speak French but Ben do. *Ben's sister doesn't speak French but*
6 How many eggs you want for breakfast? *How many eggs do you want for breakfast.*
7 Does the 9.30 train stop at every station? *RIGHT*
8 What does do your father? *What does your father do?*
9 I not write many letters. I usually use the telephone. *I don't write many letter.*
10 What Sue usually have for lunch? *What does Sue usually have for lunch.*
11 How much do these apples cost? *right*
12 Charlie plays basketball but he doesn't enjoys it. *Charlie plays basketball but he doesn't enjoy it.*

13 First, read and complete the text with phrases from the box.

~~wakes the children up~~	~~10 p.m.~~	~~a nurse~~	~~bus~~
~~20 children~~	~~6 o'clock~~	many times	~~St John's Hospital~~
~~gives them breakfast~~	very tired	~~taxi~~	

My name is Jennie. I'm (1) *a nurse* and I work at (2) *St John's Hospital*. I look after sick children at night. I start work at (3) *10 p.m.* and finish early at (4) *6 o'clock* in the morning. I go to work by (5) *bus* but I come home in the morning by (6) *taxi* because I'm tired. I have (7) *20 children* in my section. I look at the children (8) *many times* during the night. Sometimes I sit and talk to a child. The children sleep most of the time. At 6 o'clock the day nurse arrives and (9) *wakes the up*. She *children* (10) *gives them breakfast* at 7 o'clock. I go home and go to bed at 8 o'clock. I usually feel (11) *very tired*.

Now use this information to complete the questions that John asks Jennie.

12 *What do you do?*
13 Where *do you work* ?
14 What time *do you start work* ?
15 What time *do you finish* ?   *do*
16 How *you go to work* ?
17 How *do you go home* ?
18 How many *children do you have in your section* ?
19 How often *do you look at the children* ?
20 When *does the day nurse arrive* ?
21 What *does she do* at 7 o'clock?
22 How *do you usually* when you go home?

29/4

14   Paula is in the city centre. She is asking a woman some questions about her visits to the local
cinema. First, read the answers that the woman gives. Then, write the questions that Paula asks.

PAULA: (1) How often do you go to the cinema?
WOMAN: Usually once a week.
PAULA: (2) Do you go alone?
WOMAN: No, with a friend.
PAULA: (3) How do you get there?
WOMAN: I walk because I live nearby.
PAULA: (4) How much does it cost?
WOMAN: £4.00.
PAULA: (5) Where do you sit ?
WOMAN: At the back of the cinema.
PAULA: (6) What kind of films do you like
WOMAN: All kinds of films, especially comedies.
PAULA: (7) What's you favourite film?
WOMAN: My favourite is 'Silent Streets'.
PAULA: (8) Do yo buy anything, for example, ice-cream?
WOMAN: No, I don't, but I usually have a coke.
PAULA: Thank you for answering my questions.
WOMAN: You're welcome.

Now write the woman's answers in a short paragraph.

She usually (9) goes to the cinema once a week with a friend. She (10) walks to the
cinema because she (11) likes nearby. The ticket (12) lives £4.00 and
she (13) is at the back of the cinema. She (14) costs all kinds of
films, especially comedies. Her favourite film (15) doesn't eat 'Silent Streets'. She
(16) sits anything but she usually (17) buys a coke.

☺ What about you? Do you go to the cinema? Write a short paragraph like the one above:

I often go to the cinema with my mother. I go to the cinema
on foot because I live near the cinema. I like all kinds of films. And My
favourite film is 'Catch me if you can'. I usually don't eat foods in
the cinema, but I usually have a bottle of cake.

30/4

I am doing and I do (present continuous and present simple)

15 Present continuous or present simple? Complete the sentences choosing the right verb form.

1 *Do you like* learning English? (Do you like / Are you liking)
2 *I don't understand* this programme.
(I'm not understanding / I don't understand)
3 Jim and his father *aren't watching*. They are asleep.
(aren't watching / don't watch TV)
4 Tony is upstairs in the bathroom. He *is washing* his hair.
(washes / is washing)
5 Why *are we running*? Are we late? (do we run / are we running)
6 There are some strange noises in the sitting room. What *is Tom doing*?
(is Tom doing / does Tom do)
7 What time *does Tom get up* every day?
(does John get up / is John getting up)
8 Fred and I are good dancers but we *don't go* to discos very often.
(don't go / aren't going)
9 A: *Do you come* from Denmark? B: No, I'm Swedish.
(Are you coming / Do you come)
10 *I always stay* in the same hotel in New York.
(I always stay / I'm always staying)
11 *Does it snow* in winter in your country? (Does it snow / Is it snowing)
12 Joanna *isn't cooking* the dinner at the moment.
(isn't cooking / doesn't cook)
She *'s talking* on the phone. (talks / 's talking)

16 Read about what John **does** before breakfast **every day**, and what he **is doing now**.

Every day John gets up at 6.30 a.m. and does some exercises in the garden. Then he has a shower. He gets dressed and listens to the news on the radio. Then he goes downstairs and makes breakfast. At the moment, John is sitting in the kitchen and drinking a cup of tea. He is reading a magazine and thinking about his holiday.

☺ Now, you write a paragraph about yourself. Use some of the verbs below or think of your own ideas.

(a) 4 things you do before breakfast every day.
(get up / have a shower / clean my teeth / brush my hair / get dressed / do some exercises / go for a run / read / listen etc.)

and

(b) 4 things you're doing now.
(write / look (at) / drink / eat / read / sit / learn / do / think / hold / wear / work etc.)
Every day I get up at 10:00 am. And I have a shower.
At the moment I'm sitting on the bed and doing homework.

17 Complete the sentences. Put the verbs into the present simple (e.g. **do**) or present continuous (e.g. **I'm doing**), positive or negative.

1 A: Have a chocolate. B: No thank you. I _don't like chocolate._ (like chocolate)
2 A: Let's have lunch in the garden. B: No, we can't. It_'s raining._ (rain)
3 A: What _does Pam do_? B: Pam? She's a doctor. (do)
4 Tony _isn't working_ at the moment. He's on holiday. (work)
5 A: Why _are you smiling_? B: Because I'm happy. (smile)
6 Sandra and her husband are vegetarian. They _don't eat meat_. (eat meat)
7 A: What _are you reading_? B: A letter from my sister. (read)
8 A: What time _do you get up_? B: Me? About 7.00 a.m. usually. (get up)
9 A: Where's Dave? B: He's in the kitchen. He _is making coffee_. (make coffee)
10 A: How _do you go to work_? B: I usually catch a bus. (go to work)
11 A: I think Shaun and David are asleep. B: Mmm. Turn the TV off. They _aren't watching it_. (watch it)
12 John and I want to go to Greece for our holidays, so we_'re learning Greek_. (learn Greek)

18 Look at the pictures and the verbs. Write two questions for each picture. Use the present continuous for one question and the present simple for the other question.

1 RUTH: Where _are you going?_
  JAMES: To the cinema.
  RUTH: _Do you like the cinema?_
  JAMES: Yes, I do.

  (go / like)

2 YOUNG BOY: What _do you do_?
  WOMAN: I'm a photographer.
  YOUNG BOY: _What are you doing_?
  WOMAN: I'm putting a film in my camera.

  (do / do)

3 JEFF: When _do you_ usually _finish work_?
  BRIAN: At 6 o'clock.
  JEFF: Why _are you leaving_ now?
  BRIAN: Because I have a dentist's appointment.

  (finish / leave)

BRIAN

JEFF

30/4

PAUL   LUCY   JOHN

4 LUCY: What *is John doing* ?
  PAUL: Watching TV, I think.
  LUCY: *Does he watch* TV a lot?
  PAUL: Yes, every night.

              (do / watch)

LAURA
PHILLIP
£10,000

5 SUE: *What are Phillip and? Laura doing*
  TIM: Looking at a new car.
  SUE: *How much does it cost*
  TIM: £10,000.

              (do / cost)

6 BETH: *Why are they running?*
  ANNE: Because they're late.
  BETH: *What time does the?*
  ANNE: At 8.30 a.m. *school start?*

              (run / start)

---

19 Write questions and your own positive or negative short answers. Use the present simple or the present continuous.

1 you / have / dinner at the moment?
  Are you having dinner at the moment?   No, I'm not.

2 you / read / a newspaper every day?
  Do you read a newpaper every day ?   No, I don't.

3 it / snow much in your country?
  Does it snow much in your country ?   No, it isn't.

4 you / usually / do / your homework on a word processor?
  Do you usually do your homework on a ?   No, I don't.
      word procesor

5 you / drink / coffee now?
  Are you drinking coffee now. ?   No, I'm not.

6 you / drink coffee for breakfast every day?
  Do you drink coffee for breakfast every day   No, I don't.

7 you / work / at the moment?
  Are you working at the moment ?   Yes, I am.

8 children / eat lunch at school in your country?
  Do the children eat lunch at school ?   No, they don't.
  in your country

10

have got

20 Complete the story about Ruth. Put in **has got** ('s got), **have got** ('ve got), **hasn't got** or **haven't got**.

Ruth is 21. She (1) _has got_ fair hair and blue eyes. She (2) _'s got_ two brothers, William and Phillip, but she (3) _hasn't got_ any sisters. Her brothers (4) _have got_ brown hair and brown eyes. One of her brothers, Phillip, is married and (5) _has got_ two children, so she's an aunt. Ruth lives with her parents in an apartment. It (6) _has got_ five rooms but it (7) _hasn't got_ a garden. She (8) _has got_ her own room in the apartment. In it she (9) _has got_ her computer and a TV. She (10) _has got_ a car but her parents (11) _haven't got_ one because they can't drive.

☺ What about you? What have you got? Look at Ruth's story and then write about yourself.

hair / eyes? _I've got thick hair and black eyes._
brothers / sisters / parents etc.? _I've not got any brothers or sisters._
house / apartment? _____
computer / car / bicycle / a lot of books etc.? _____

21 Write questions. Use **have you got, has it got …?** etc.

1 MARY: Tim is a good photographer.
  PAT: What kind of camera _has he got?_
2 STUART: I'm rich!
  VAL: How much money _have you got_?
3 TONY: Kate is going to the dentist this afternoon.
  ALICE: _Has he got_ toothache?
4 DEREK: Jane and Jim are buying a new house.
  PETER: How many rooms _have they got_?
5 DIANA: Tony wants to talk to you.
  ALEX: _Has he got_ my telephone number?
6 MARTIN: My sister and brother-in-law have been married for six years.
  ROSE: _Have they got_ any children?
7 HELEN: My neighbours love cats.
  PAM: How many _cat have they got_
8 LAURA: My bag is very heavy.
  ADAM: What _has it got_ in it?

22 Put in **has got** ('s got), ('ve got). Use the positive, negative or question forms.

1 Those flowers are really beautiful and they _'ve got_ a wonderful smell.
2 I must write down John's telephone number. _Have you got_ a pen?
3 Mary works very hard so she _has got_ time for many hobbies.
4 New York _has got_ a very interesting modern art museum.
5 I can't show you the photographs because I _haven't got_ them with me.
6 Tigers _'ve got_ strange, yellow eyes.
7 'What kind of Walkman _has_ Carol _got_?' 'A Sony, I think.'

11

was/were and I worked/got/went etc. (past simple)

23 Complete the sentences. Use **I/she was** etc. or **we/they were** etc.

1 Liz worked very late last night.   *She was* tired.
2 Jack lost his job yesterday.   He was angry.
3 We laughed a lot at last night's film.   It was very funny.
4 Joe and Sam fell into the river yesterday.   They were wet and cold.
5 Yesterday was a beautiful day.   It was sunny.
6 We saw a horror film last Saturday.   We were really frightened.
7 David and Sue didn't have anything to eat yesterday.   They were hungry.
8 I had a wonderful holiday last year.   I was happy.

24 Where were you at these times? Use **I was at/in** + a place.

🙂 1 *I was at the swimming pool* at 6.30 yesterday morning.
2 I was in the shopping centre last Saturday.
3 I was at home at 7 o'clock yesterday evening.
4 I was at Denise's home last Tuesday afternoon.
5 I was at my room at midnight last night.
6 I was in the shopping centre at 1 o'clock yesterday.
7 I was in my room ten minutes ago.

25 Write questions with **was/were** + the words in brackets ( ), and give short answers.

1 MAX: My grandmother died in 1976.
  OSCAR: *Was she very old?* (old)
  MAX: No, she wasn't.

2 ELSA: James and Ruth had an oral examination yesterday
  BETH: Was it difficult? (difficult)
  ELSA: No, it wasn't.

3 SALLY: I had a little red sports car in 1993.
  TONY: Was it fast? (fast)
  SALLY: Yes, it was.

4 DAVE: Mike got some tickets for the World Cup.
  SUE: Were they expensive (expensive)
  DAVE: No, they weren't

5 ALAN: I didn't like school when I was young.
  KATE: Were you lazy? (lazy)
  ALAN: No, I wasn't.

6 BEN: Julia wasn't at work yesterday.
  MARK: Was she ill? (ill)
  BEN: Yes, she was.

7 RUTH: My grandfather met the comedians Laurel and Hardy in 1950.
  TOM: Were they famous? (famous)
  RUTH: Yes, they were

26   Look at the pictures and complete the sentences in the correct form of the past simple. Use the verb in brackets ( ).

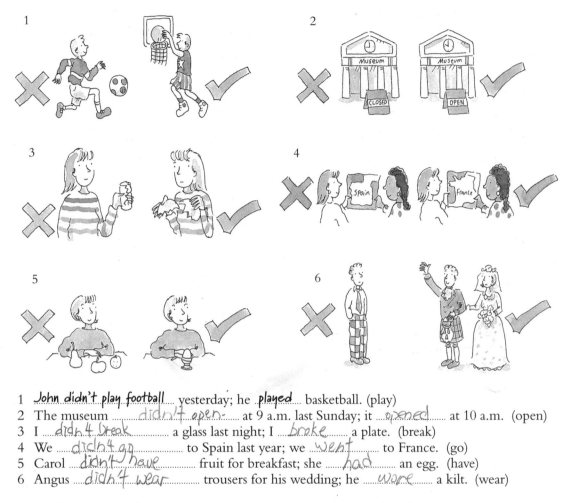

1 *John didn't play football* yesterday; he **played** basketball. (play)
2 The museum _didn't open_ at 9 a.m. last Sunday; it _opened_ at 10 a.m. (open)
3 I _didn't break_ a glass last night; I _broke_ a plate. (break)
4 We _didn't go_ to Spain last year; we _went_ to France. (go)
5 Carol _didn't have_ fruit for breakfast; she _had_ an egg. (have)
6 Angus _didn't wear_ trousers for his wedding; he _wore_ a kilt. (wear)

Look at these pictures. Complete the sentences with a past simple verb in the negative.

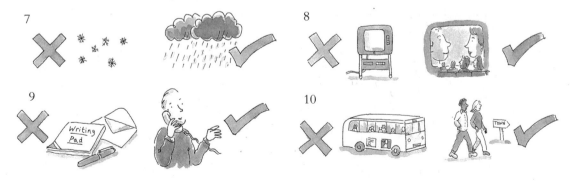

7 It _didn't snow_ much last winter; it rained a lot.
8 Barbara and Charlie _didn't watch TV_ last night; they went to the cinema.
9 Tim _didn't write_ to his parents last week; he telephoned them.
10 We _didn't travel by bus_ to the city centre; we walked.

27　A father asked his child some questions at the end of the day. Write the questions using **Did you …**
　　with a verb from box A, and choose an ending from box B.

A		B	
~~go~~	~~have~~	a big lunch	any money
play	~~watch~~	volleyball	your grandmother
~~have~~	do	~~school~~	your homework
visit	spend	a history lesson	your favourite TV programme

25/5

1　Did you go to school?
2　Did you have a big lunch ?
3　Did you play volleyball ?
4　Did you visit your grandmother ?
5　Did you do your homework ?
6　Did you spend any money ?
7　Did you watch your favourite TV programme ?
8　Did you have a history lesson ?

28　First, complete the story of Maria's day. Choose from the list below. Then, write the questions that you
　　asked Maria.

~~spaghetti~~	~~1 p.m.~~	~~the sports centre~~	~~9 a.m.~~	~~an Italian restaurant~~	~~8 a.m.~~
~~half an hour later~~	~~my brother~~	~~a birthday present~~	~~bus~~	~~did some work~~	

I left home at (1) **8 a.m.** yesterday morning and went to college by (2) bus.
I arrived there (3) half an hour later. My lessons began at (4) 9.am
and finished at (5) 1 pm. I went to (6) an Italian restaurant for
lunch. I met (7) my brother there and we had lunch together. We both ate
(8) spaghetti. After lunch, I bought (9) a birthday present for
my father, and my brother went to (10) the sports centre to play volleyball. In the
evening I stayed at home and (11) did some work.

Now complete the questions that you asked Maria.

12　When **did you leave home?**
13　How did you get there ?
14　When did you get home ?
15　What time did you go to school ?
16　What time did your brother get there ?
17　Where did you go ?
18　Who did you meet ?
19　What did you do ?
20　What did you eat ?
21　Where did your brother go ?
22　What did your brother do ?

29 Put in **had**, **didn't have** or **Did ... have?**

1 When I was a student I was always poor. I _didn't have much money._   26/15
2 A: I arrived home very late yesterday. B: _Did you have_ a lot of work to do at your office?
3 Ann couldn't go to Moscow last week because she _didn't have_ the correct visa.
4 When my brother and I were children, we _had_ two dogs and a cat.
5 _Didn't_ Sue _have_ a problem with her TV last night?
6 Not many people _had_ cars in the 1920s.
7 A: The customs officers at Chicago airport stopped my parents when they arrived.
   B: What _did they have_ in their suitcases?
   A: Nothing – only their personal things.

30 A postcard from New York. Complete this postcard that Tony received from his friend Helen. Use a verb in the past simple (e.g. **arrived**) or **was/were**. One verb is in the negative.

> Hi Tony!
>
> I'm in San Francisco now. We (1) _arrived_ here yesterday. Before that, we
> (2) _stayed_ 10 days in New York. It (3) _was_ wonderful. Pat and I
> (4) _saw_ a lot of interesting places including the Empire State Building. We
> (5) _went_ to the top – it (6) _was_ very high, and we
> (7) _were_ both a bit frightened. We (8) _took_ a boat along the river to
> see the Statue of Liberty. We (9) _went_ through Greenwich Village and
> watched many artists at work. The paintings (10) _were not_ expensive so I
> bought one. We also (11) _went_ to the theatre and saw a new musical – I
> (12) _loved_ it very much. The weather (13) _was_ OK – a bit wet
> sometimes. But now in San Francisco, it's hot and sunny.
> See you soon.
> Love Helen (and Pat)

☺ Now, you write a postcard to a friend from your last holiday place.

> Dear Sally,
>   I'm in Gram now. We arrived here yesterday.
> It's wonderful here. I went to many beautiful
> places. For example, k-mark, and Ftcory-outlet. We bought
> a lot of things, I am happy!
>
> See you soon.
>
> Love from,
>
> Donna

31 Two friends meet after the weekend. Alice had a good weekend but Tim didn't. Write the other half of the conversation. (Read Alice's answers first.)

TIM: How are you?
ALICE: (1) ..(I'm) fine, thanks...
TIM: Did you have a good weekend?
ALICE: (2) ....Yes, I did...
TIM: Did you enjoy the film?
ALICE: (3) ....It was........... excellent.
TIM: What did you do after that?
ALICE: (4) ....I had dinner.......
TIM: That sounds nice. What was the food like?
ALICE: (5) ....Good......., but ....it was.... too much! What about you?
        How was your weekend?
TIM: (6) Terrible! .... with the car.
ALICE: Oh dear! I'm sorry to hear that. Are you all right?
TIM: Yes, I'm fine now but I (7) ...had............. a bad headache for two days.
ALICE: And what about the car? Was there a lot of damage?
TIM: It wasn't too bad. The garage (8) .... and I can drive it again now.
ALICE: Oh, well. Come and have some lunch with me and forget about the weekend.

18/6

I was doing and I did
(past continuous and past simple)

32 Look at the picture. This was the scene in Rosamund Street at 10.30 a.m. yesterday. Write what was happening and where it was happening. Use the past continuous.

1 Felix was sleeping on a car.
2 Phillip was reading the newspaper.
3 Rosa was using the computer.
4 Paul was .... the car.
5 Sam's dogs was running.
6 Mrs Drake was buying something.

7   Sam was climbing a tree.
8   Lynn was lying.
9   Mike and Tim was waiting for a bus.   9/6

☺ And you? What were you doing yesterday at …? Use the past continuous.

10   10.30 a.m.   At 10.30 a.m. yesterday I was sleeping.
11   12.30 p.m.   At 12:30 pm yesterday I was waiting for my friend
12   4.00 p.m.   At 4:00pm yesterday I was at school.
13   8.30 p.m.   At 8:30pm yesterday I was watching TV.
14   1.00 a.m.   At 1:00am yesterday I was sleeping.

33 Complete the conversations. Use **was/were**, or use the past simple (**I did**, etc.) or the past continuous (**was doing**, etc.) of the verb in brackets ( ).

1   POLICEMAN: What were you doing (you / do) when the accident happened (happen)?
   COLIN: I was at the bus-stop. I was waiting (wait) for a bus.
   POLICEMAN: Did you see (you / see) the accident?
   COLIN: No, because I was reading (read) the newspaper.

2   NICOLA: I telephoned (telephone) you at 9 o'clock last night but you were not at home.
   MARTIN: 9 o'clock? I was sitting (sit) in a café, drinking (drink) hot chocolate.
   NICOLA: Was Jane with you?
   MARTIN: No, she worked (work) in the library.
   NICOLA: Where did you go (you / go) after the café?
   MARTIN: I went (go) home.

3   MUM: Oh no! My beautiful new plate. What happened?
   ANGELA: I'm really sorry, Mum. I broke (break) it when I was washing (wash) it.
   MUM: How?
   ANGELA: My hands were wet and I dropped (drop) it on the floor.

4   SOPHIE: Do you think (you / think) yesterday's exam was difficult?
   EDWARD: No, not really, but I didn't write (not / write) very much.
   SOPHIE: Why not?
   EDWARD: Because I dreamed (dream) about my holidays.

5   ANDREW: There was a crash outside my house yesterday.
   PIPPA: What happened (happen)?
   ANDREW: I don't know. It was raining (rain) but the drivers didn't go (not / go) fast.
   PIPPA: Were they hurt?
   ANDREW: One man broke (break) his arm and the other man cut (cut) his head.

6   TRACY: Pardon? I didn't hear you. Could you repeat that, please?
   NEIL: I wasn't talking (not / talk) to you.
   TRACY: Who were you talking (you / talk) to?
   NEIL: Sarah.
   TRACY: Oh, sorry.

34   At 10.05 a.m. yesterday, there was a robbery at the Midwest Bank. You are a police officer and you are asking a man some questions about what he was doing, what other people were doing, and what he saw. Write the questions. Use **was/were**, the past simple (**did you …**) and the past continuous (**were you …**).

TIM
SMITH

MRS WALTERS

MRS JONES

'Now then, Mr Smith, I know you saw the robbery yesterday. I would like to ask you to some questions. First of all, …

1   What / you / do / at 10.05 a.m. yesterday?
    What were you doing at 10.05 a.m. yesterday?
2   Where / be / Joan Turner?   *Where was Joan Turner at 10:05am?*
3   What / Mrs Jones / do? ....?
4   Where / Mrs Walters / go? ....?
5   How many robbers / go / into the bank?
    ....?
6   they / carry / guns? ....?
7   Where / the big car / wait? ....?
8   driver / a man or a woman? ....?
9   you / see / a man in an old jacket on the corner?
    ....?
10   some men / repair / the road? ....?
11   anyone / wait / at the bus stop? ....?

Thank you, Mr Smith, that was very helpful.'

Now write Mr Smith's answers into a paragraph. Look at the picture to help you find the information.

Mr Smith told me that at 10.05 a.m. yesterday she (12) *was ouside the butcher's.* Joan Turner
(13) .... Mrs Jones (14) .... with her dog.
Mrs Walters (15) .... (16) .... robbers ....
the bank and they (17) .... guns. A big car (18) ....
and the driver (19) .... A man in an old jacket (20) ....
and some men (21) .... the road. Two children (22) ....
at the bus-stop.

Review (present and past, simple and continuous)

35 Look at this information about Marco and Jill.

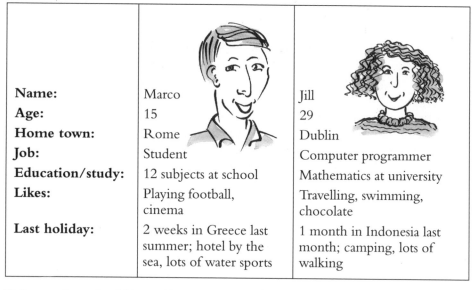

	Marco	Jill
Name:	Marco	Jill
Age:	15	29
Home town:	Rome	Dublin
Job:	Student	Computer programmer
Education/study:	12 subjects at school	Mathematics at university
Likes:	Playing football, cinema	Travelling, swimming, chocolate
Last holiday:	2 weeks in Greece last summer; hotel by the sea, lots of water sports	1 month in Indonesia last month; camping, lots of walking

Write questions about Marco. Use a verb in the present or past.

1   _How old is Marco?_ (old?)
2   _Where does he live?_ (live?)
3   .... (do?)
4   .... (study?)
5   .... (like?)
6   .... (last holiday?)
7   .... (stay?)
8   .... (do on holiday?)

Read the paragraph about Marco.

Marco is 15 and he comes from Rome. He is a student and is studying 12 subjects at school. He likes playing football and going to the cinema. Last summer he went to Greece for 2 weeks. He stayed in a hotel by the sea and he played lots of water sports.

Write a similar paragraph for Jill.

9 Jill is ....
   ....
   ....

☺ Now do the same for yourself.

I am ....
   ....
   ....

36 Complete the conversations. Put the verb in the correct form in the present or past.

1 JIM: (1) *Were* you *going* (go) shopping when I saw you yesterday morning?
   KATE: No, I (2) *was* on my way to the bank.
   JIM: I (3) *go* (go) to the bank every Friday, before the weekend.
   KATE: Me too usually. But this week I (4) *didn't have* (not / have) time, so I (5) *went* (go)
           yesterday.

2 JAN: (6) .... you .... (see) that science programme on TV last
           night?
   SAM: No, (7) .... never .... (watch) TV.
   JAN: It (8) .... wonderful. It (9) .... (show) a new way of repairing a
           heart.
   SAM: Oh.

3 JILL: Why (10) .... you .... (look) at me?
   TONY: Because you (11) .... (wear) a new dress and you look very good in
           it.
   JILL: Thank you. I (12) .... (buy) it yesterday.

4 VAL: What (13) .... Jim .... (do) this morning?
   IAN: He's at the doctor's at the moment.
   VAL: Oh dear. What (14) .... (happen)?
   IAN: He (15) .... (fall) and (16) .... (hurt) his leg yesterday when he
           (17) .... (run) for a bus.

5 VIC: (18) .... Sally .... (work) at half past seven last night?
   PAM: No, she (19) .... (help) me with the dinner. She often
           (20) .... (help) in the kitchen.
   VIC: When (21) .... she .... (go) out?
   PAM: She didn't. She (22) .... (stay) at home all evening.

37 Complete this conversation with a famous film actor. Put the verb into the correct form of the past or
present.

INTERVIEWER: When (1) *did you start* (you / start) acting?
ACTOR: When I (2) .... (be) 12. I (3) .... (go) to a drama
              school, and one day I (4) .... (sit) in the classroom and Nigel
              Stewart, the famous film director, (5) .... (visit) the school. He
              (6) .... (see) me, and that (7) .... (be) the
              beginning.
INTERVIEWER: What (8) .... (be) your first film?
ACTOR: 'Holiday Home' with Terry Veale, who (9) .... (be) now my
              husband! We (10) .... (make) the film in Italy. He
              (11) .... (be) 17 and I (12) .... (be) 13!
INTERVIEWER: I know that Terry Veale (13) .... (have) an accident in that film.
              How (14) .... (it / happen)?
ACTOR: Well, one day near the end of the filming we (15) .... (both /
              ride) horses and Terry's horse suddenly (16) .... (stop) and he
              (17) .... (fall) off. He (18) .... (break) his arm.
              Today, Terry and I often (19) .... (talk) about our first meeting.
INTERVIEWER: (20) .... (you / ride) nowadays?
ACTOR: No, I (21) .... (stop) when I (22) .... (move) to Los
              Angeles.

INTERVIEWER: I know you are very busy but what (23) .... (you / do) in your
               free time?
ACTOR: Terry and I (24) .... (like) swimming. We (25) ....
               (swim) every day. And of course, I (26) .... (love) cooking. The
               dish I (27) .... (make) for lunch today is a new idea of mine.
INTERVIEWER: Can I ask you some more questions? And can I also talk to Terry?
ACTOR: Yes, of course. He (28) .... (swim) in our pool at the moment. We
               can go outside and enjoy the sun. Come on.

I have done (present perfect)

38   Complete the sentences. Use the present perfect in the correct form.

1 A: Is it raining at the moment? B: _No, it's just stopped_ (it / just / stop).
2 I can't find my keys. _Have you seen_ (you / see) them?
3 A: Where's your dictionary?
   B: I don't know .... (it / disappear).
4 A: Let's go and see 'Lions of Africa' at the Cannon cinema.
   B: .... (I / already / see) it.
   A: Oh well, ... (you / see) 'Green Beans'?
   B: No, let's go to that.
5 A: Please can I have my book back.
   B: Oh dear. .... (I / not / finish) it.
6 A: Are Steve and Martha at home? B: No, ... (they / go) out.
7 John looks thinner. .... (he / lose) weight?
8 A: Is Sally enjoying her new job?
   B: I don't know. .... (I / not / hear) from her.
9 A: Why doesn't this tape recorder work?
   B: I think .... (you / break) it.
10 Mary, you're very late. I was worried about you. Where ....
   (you / be)?
11 A: How many times .... (you / take) your driving test?
   B: Twice. My third one is next week.
12 This music is new to me. I'm sure .... (I / not / hear) it before.

39 Complete the sentences with **already** (I've already ... / She's already ...) or **yet** (He hasn't ... yet / They haven't ... yet).

1 MARK: Let's go to the new Spielman exhibition at the Modern Art Museum.
   JANE: I've already seen it. It's not very good. (see)

2 DAVID: Don't forget to tell Mary the good news.
   LIZ: I .... and she was very happy. (tell)

3 SUE: What does John say in his letter?
   CHRIS: I don't know. I .... I've been too busy. (read)

4 TIM: Did Sue's operation go well?
   PAT: She .... The hospital were too busy. (have)

5 JOHN: I enjoyed reading that new novel by Sarah Dunmore. Is it her first book?
   JILL: No, she .... three, but I think this one is her best. (write)

6 PETE: Is that your father's new car?
   PAUL: Yes, it arrived last week but he .... (drive)

7 KATE: When are Tony and Chris going to sell their house?
   MICK: They .... They're moving to London next week. (sell)

40 You work for a travel agency. A customer, Jack, is interested in one of your walking holidays in the tropical rain forests of South America. You are asking him some questions beginning **Have you ever ...?**

YOU:	JACK:
1 Can you walk a long distance?	Yes, no problem.
Have you ever walked (walk) more than 40 kms?	Yes, often.
2 Are you healthy?	Yes, very.
.... (have) a serious illness?	No, never.
.... (break) an arm or a leg?	My leg, twice.
3 Can you swim?	Yes.
.... (travel) in a canoe?	Yes, once.
4 Do you like flying?	Not very much.
.... (fly) in a helicopter?	Yes, a few times.
5 Can you read a map?	I think so.
.... (lose) your way?	No, never.
6 Do you sleep well?	Yes, always.
.... (sleep) outside?	Yes, many times.
7 Are you afraid of heights?	No.
.... (climb) a high mountain?	Yes, once.

Now write 3 sentences saying what Jack has done, and 3 sentences saying what Jack hasn't done

Jack has done a lot of things at different times in his life.
  He has (often) walked more than 40 kms, ...
but
  He has never ridden an elephant or a camel, ...

☺ And what about you?

  I've never walked more than 40 kms. ....

41 Put in **has/have been** or **has/have gone**.

1 HARRY: I saw you in Annabel's Restaurant last night
  DIANA: No, it wasn't me. I've never _been_ there.

2 SAM: Sally and Tim are on holiday, aren't they? Where .... they ....?
  SUE: To Florida, again.
  SAM: How many times .... they .... there?
  SUE: This is their third visit.

3 JOE: Can I have an apple, please?
  MARY: We haven't got any. I ....n't .... to the shops today.

4 ALAN: Where's Tony?
  MARK: He's got a headache so he .... to bed.

5 STEVE: (*on the phone*) Can I speak to Jill, please?
  LYNN: She's out, I'm afraid. She .... to the cinema this evening.
  STEVE: Again? She .... already .... to the cinema three times this week.

42 Complete the sentences using verbs in the present perfect.

'See that man over there? I'm sure I (1) _'ve seen_ him on TV. Oh yes, I remember, it's
David Sen – the man I'm going to see at the Festival Hall tonight. He's a wonderful piano
player. He and his family (2) .... a lot of different things in their lives. He
(3) .... all over the world and he (4) .... many interesting
people. He (5) .... a lot of money in piano-playing competitions so he's rich
now. His daughter's only 20 and she (6) .... already .... a very
successful cookery book and she's writing another one now. That's his son, Kenny, with
him. He loves motorbikes. He (7) .... his bike all the way from Canada to
Chile and he (8) .... just .... the story of his journey to a travel magazine.
So *he'll* also be rich soon!
David Sen's wife is a musician, too. She plays the flute. They (9) ....
together many times in different countries. But they (10) .... never .... to
our town before, so I'm going to their concert at the Festival Hall tonight.'
'You certainly know a lot about him!'

How long have you ...? (present perfect)

43 Complete the conversations. Make questions with **How long ...** + the present perfect simple.

1 PIPPA: Do you like London?
   MARTIN: Yes, very much.
   PIPPA: *How long have you lived* here? (live)

2 MIKE: This is a really good party, isn't it?
   JEAN: Yes, great.
   MIKE: .... here? (be)

3 PETE: Does Julie enjoy her work?
   LYNN: Not very much. She thinks the bank is a bit boring.
   PETE: .... there? (work)

4 TOM: Are you OK? You look a bit pale.
   LIZ: I've got a headache.
   TOM: .... it? (have)

5 ALEX: Did you know David and Sheila are going to get married in the autumn?
   JOHN: .... each other? (know)

6 SARAH: Today is Tom's last day at work. He doesn't want to stop but he's 65 next month so ...
   DAVID: .... with his company? (be)
   SARAH: All his working life.

44 **Since** or **for**? Put the following words and phrases into sentence 1 or sentence 2.

his birthday	~~Monday~~	more than 2 years	he left school
~~3 hours~~	a long time	this morning	2 o'clock yesterday
the beginning of April	Christmas	4 months	6 weeks 1992

1 Tony has worked here since ...   *Monday* ....
   ....
   ....

2 John has been married for ...   *3 hours* ....
   ....
   ....

45 Complete the sentences with a time phrase + **ago** (e.g. **2 hours ago**) or **for** + a time phrase (e.g. **for ten minutes**).

1 You can't be hungry. You had lunch *half an hour ago.*
2 Jane is fed up. She's been waiting *for a bus for an hour.*
3 I don't live in London now. I moved to New York ....
4 I now live in New York. I've been here ....
5 Tom's grandparents died ....
6 Tims got 'flu. He's been in bed ....
7 Jane and William got married .... and their first child was born
   ....
8 I like Mary's hair. She's had it in that style ....

46   Write a sentence for each situation. Use present perfect continuous (**has/have been doing**, etc.) + **for** or **since**.

1 John started his phone call twenty minutes ago and he is still talking.
    John _has been talking for twenty minutes._

2 Sam and I arranged to meet at the cinema at 7.00 p.m. I arrived on time but I'm still waiting for Sam to arrive.
    I ....

3 Barbara and Kevin are tired. They started walking six hours ago and they're still walking.
    They ....

4 You started watching TV at 9 o'clock this morning and you're still watching it.
    You ....

5 I hate this weather! It started raining last week and it's still raining.
    It ....

6 Laura felt sick at lunchtime today and she is still feeling sick.
    Laura ....

7 Six months ago Colin and I started building our own house. We're still doing it.
    We ....

8 Fred got on the Trans–European express train on June 28th. Today is 1st July and he is still travelling.
    Fred ....

I have done and **I did** (present perfect and past simple)

47   Write questions. Use the present perfect or the past simple. Look at the answers before you write the questions.

1 How long / Sarah / live / in France?
    How long has Sarah lived in France ?   Since 1990.

2 When / John / lose his job?
    .... ?   3 weeks ago.

3 When / the last time / you / have / a holiday?
    .... ?   Last year.

4 How long / Jill / have a cat?
    .... ?   Since January.

5 What time / you / finish work?
    .... ?   At 9.00 p.m.

6 How long / you / watch TV / last night?
    .... ?   All evening.

7 When / Chris / go out?
    .... ?   Ten minutes ago.

8 How long / your father / in hospital?
    .... ?   Since Monday.

48 Write complete sentences. Use the present perfect and the past simple.

1 You / be / tired / all day. What time / you / go to bed / last night?
 You've been tired all day. What time did you go to bed last night?

2 Francis / leave / home / 6 o'clock this morning. He / drive / since then.
 Francis left home at 6 o'clock this morning. He has been driving since then.

3 Brasilia / the capital of Brazil / since 1960. Before 1960, Rio de Janeiro / the capital.
 ....

4 Carol / move / to Oxford / in 1975. She / live / in Oxford / since 1975.
 ....

5 I / not / see / the new manager / yet. When / she / start working for the company?
 ....

6 You / speak / good French / on the telephone / yesterday. How long / you / learn / it?
 ....

7 Paula and Laurence / be / married / since last year. They / meet / at university.
 ....

8 Peter / never / try / Japanese food. He / go Japan / last year but he / eat / hamburgers.
 ....

9 I / break my arm / six months ago. I / use / a computer for my work / since then.
 ....

10 My brother / be / a professional footballer / since 1994. But when he / be / younger he /
 not / like / sport very much.
 ....

49 Put the verb in the present perfect or the past simple.

Here is the six o'clock news from ITC, on Monday the 25th April.
Our reporter in Nepal (1) *telephoned* (telephone) us ten minutes ago and (2) *said* (say) that
Jane Tomkins and her partner, Ann Beckett, are on top of the world today. They
(3) .... (reach) the top of Mount Everest half hour ago. Our reporter spoke
to another climber on the expedition.
REPORTER: Are Jane and Ann still on the top of Mount Everest?
CLIMBER: No, they (4) .... (start) their return journey.
REPORTER: How long (5) .... they .... (spend) up there?
CLIMBER: About 10 minutes. They (6) .... (take) some photographs of
 each other.
REPORTER: Are they in good health?
CLIMBER: Well, they're both tired, but they're fine. But there is one problem: the weather
 (7) .... (change). There is more cloud and the wind is quite
 strong.

Last night, Manchester United (8) .... (win) the football league championship. The team (9) .... (win) the championship three times now – the first time (10) .... (be) in 1986. In their final game yesterday, Bryan Riggs (11) .... (score) the winning goal. Riggs (12) .... (be) with the team since he (13) .... (leave) school.

The President of Volponia, Madame Fernoff, (14) .... (arrive) in Britain last night. Madame Fernoff (15) .... (be) President since 1985. She said she was very happy to be in Britain.

At yesterday's meeting of European finance ministers, Jack Delaney, the Irish Finance Minister, (16) .... (say), 'I am going to leave my job soon. I (17) .... (work) very hard and I want to spend more time with my family.' Mr Delaney (18) .... (be) Irish Finance Minister for 5 years.

And the weather. We (19) .... (have) a lot of rain over the country since the beginning of the week and unfortunately this will continue until the weekend. For your information, last week (20) .... (be) the wettest April week for 100 years.

---

50   Complete the dialogues. Use the present perfect or the past simple of the verbs in brackets ( ).

1 CLARE: *Have* you *seen* (see) John?
   COLIN: No, why?
   CLARE: He*'s broken* (break) his leg.
   COLIN: Really? When *did* he *do* (do) that?
   CLARE: Yesterday.

2 ADAM: Oh no! I .... (lose) my car keys.
   TONY: When .... you last .... (see) them?
   ADAM: This morning when I .... (leave) the house.

3 MARY: Alan's going to sell his car.
   SIMON: Really? He only .... (buy) it last month.
   MARY: I know. He loves changing cars.
   SIMON: How many cars .... he .... (have) in his life?
   MARY: At least 20!

4 BEN: Can I look at the newspaper, please?
   VAL: In a minute. I .... (not / finish) with it yet.
   BEN: You're very slow. You .... (start) it this morning after breakfast!

5 JULIA: There was a good programme on TV last night about elephants.
             .... you .... (see) it?
   SARAH: Yes, it was wonderful. .... you ever .... (see) a *live* elephant?
   JULIA: Yes, and I .... (touch) one, too.
   SARAH: When .... (be) that?
   JULIA: Two years ago when I .... (be) on holiday in Kenya.

6 PATRICK: Connie looks really fed up. What's the matter?
   JOSIE: She .... (fail) her driving test yesterday.
   PATRICK: Not again! How many times .... she .... (fail)?
   JOSIE: I think it's four.

Review (present, present perfect and past)

51 Follow the instructions for each exercise.

A Choose the right answer.

At 11 o'clock yesterday morning, John (1) <u>was</u> / <s>has been</s> sitting in the waiting room at the doctor's. Next to him (2) <u>is/was</u> a woman with a very large thumb. (3) 'How <u>did you do / were you doing</u> that?' John asked. (4) 'I <u>hung / was hanging</u> a picture on the wall and I (5) <u>hit / was hitting</u> my thumb by mistake.' (6) 'Oh dear. How long (6) <u>have you been / are you</u> waiting for the doctor?' 'About an hour, and my thumb (7) <u>is hurting / has hurt</u> a lot.'

B Put the verb in brackets ( ) in the correct tense.

Mary usually (8) ..<u>takes</u>.. (take) a bus to the office but today she (9) .... (drive) because she is late. Last night her manager (10) .... (telephone) her and (11) .... (ask) her to be at the office at 8.30 a.m. for an important meeting. 'I (12) .... late (never / be) for a meeting in my life. Why (13) .... (my mother / forget) to wake me this morning?'

C Complete the questions.

MARK: (14) **What's** your job?
PETE: I'm an engineer with National Telephones.
MARK: How long (15) .... for that company?
PETE: About 9 months.
MARK: (16) .... it?
PETE: No, not really. I preferred my old job.
MARK: What (17) .... that?
PETE: I was a gardener.

CHRIS: (18) .... ever .... an accident?
ANNE: Yes, once a few years ago.
CHRIS: How (19) ....?
ANNE: I was driving too fast.
CHRIS: (20) .... a bad accident?
ANNE: Not very bad. I broke my arm but the other driver was OK.
CHRIS: Why (21) .... fast now?
ANNE: I'm not! This is my normal speed in a town.

TOM: Why (22) .... at me?
RUTH: Because you've got a bit of tomato on your face.
TOM: Where (23) .... it?
RUTH: On the right of your nose.
TOM: (24) .... or is it still there?
RUTH: It's still there.

52 Read the letter from Chris to her friend, Jo. Chris is from San Francisco and has just had a holiday with Jo in London. Complete the sentences. Put the verb in brackets in the correct form.

Dear Jo

Well, I (1) arrived (arrive) *back safely two weeks ago. The flight* (2) .... (be) *fine, but a bit long. I* (3) .... (watch) *two films and* (4) .... (eat) *two breakfasts!*

Thank you for everything. I (5) .... (have) *a really good time with you in London. I hope you* (6) .... (enjoy) *it too.*

Everything here is very different from London. I (7) .... (write) *this letter outside in the garden. I* (8) .... (sit) *under a big umbrella because the sun is very hot today. I know we* (9) .... (have) *some sunny days in London but I remember there* (10) .... (be) *also some rain!*

It was difficult for me to start work after my wonderful holiday, but it's OK now. I (11) .... (be) *in a new department since I* (12) .... (come) *home and it's interesting. I* (13) .... (have) *a new manager now, and that's good because the old one* (14) .... (be) *horrible.*

(15) .... (you / like) *rock music? My brother* (16) .... (be) *a drummer in a new group. He* (17) .... (practise) *in his bedroom at the moment and it's quite loud! I* (18) .... (just / send) *you some of his cassettes. I hope you like them.*

By the way, (19) .... (you / find) *a black leather photo album? I think I* (20) .... (leave) *it in the bedroom. Could you send it to me sometime? No hurry.*

Jill (21) .... (sit) *in the garden with me and she sends her love to you. Please write soon, and thank you again for a wonderful time.*

Love Chris

Now write Jo's reply in complete sentences.

Dear Chris

22 Thank you for your letter. Yes, I / enjoy / the time you / spend / with me very much. We / have / some good fun!
   Thank you for your letter. Yes, I enjoyed the time ....
   ....

23 You / leave / a wonderful box of chocolates for my parents. Thank you. We / just / finish / them – they / be delicious.
   ....
   ....

24 And thank you also for the cassettes. They / arrive / yesterday. I / not / play / all of them yet. At the moment I / listen / to one, 'Paradise Rock'. It / be / very good.
   ....
   ....

→

25 My mother / find / your photo album the day you / leave. I / send / it back two weeks ago. you / receive / it yet?

....

26 Do you remember Steve? We / meet / him at Sue's party. Well, he / come / to my house last week. He / ask / for your address so I / give / it to him. I hope that's OK. He / be / in California now on business.

....

27 I / look / out of the window at the moment. The sun / shine and it / be / a beautiful, warm day. In fact, it / be / sunny / every day since you / go back / to San Francisco. Sorry!

....

28 The cassette / just / finish. Tell your brother I love his music. he / want / a publicity agent in London?

....

That's all for now. Write soon.
Love
Jo

☺ Last week you stayed with a friend for a few days, but now you are home again. Write a 'thank you' letter to the friend. Use the following points and the letter from Chris to Jo to help you.

- thank the friend
- write about the journey home
- write about the things you enjoyed when you were with your friend
- you are sending a present – tell / him her about it
- write what you're doing now
- ask her / him to write to you

---

is done / was done and is being done / has been done (passive)

53 Write the quiz questions. Use the past simple passive.

QUIZ MASTER: Welcome to our General Knowledge Quiz. We've got some interesting questions for you tonight, Marianne, so are you ready?

MARIANNE: Ready.

QUIZ MASTER: OK, number 1: When (1) _was_ the toothbrush _invented_ (invent)? Was it the 15th or the 17th century?

MARIANNE: The 15th century, I think – in China.

QUIZ MASTER: That's right. Number 2: Where (2) .... compact discs .... (develop)?

MARIANNE: In Japan.

QUIZ MASTER: Japan and The Netherlands together, actually. And number 3: (3) .... dynamite .... (invent) in Canada, Sweden or Greece?

MARIANNE:	In Sweden by Alfred Nobel.
QUIZ MASTER:	OK, Number 4: in which century (4) .... glasses first .... (make)?
MARIANNE:	I'm not sure. The 15th century?
QUIZ MASTER:	No, I'm sorry. It was in the 13th century by two Italians. And for your fifth question: When (5) .... contact lenses first .... (produce)?
MARIANNE:	1956.
QUIZ MASTER:	Correct. And your last question: Where (6) .... the first petrol car ....? (build)
MARIANNE:	In Germany by Mr Daimler and Mr Benz.
QUIZ MASTER:	That's right. Congratulations, Marianne. You did very well.

54 Look at the picture of Hartson's jam factory. A visitor is being shown around the factory by Mr Jones, the manager. Complete his sentences. Use the passive (present simple or continuous).

The machines (1) **are switched on** (switch on) at 7.30 a.m. every day and (2) **(are) turned off** (turn off) at 5.30 p.m. The factory (3) .... (lock) at 6.30 p.m. by our security guards and all the staff (4) .... (check) before they go home. We don't want our jam to disappear! Now as you can see, strawberry jam (5) .... (make) here today. And over there the jars of jam (6) .... (put) into boxes by our team. Hartson's jam (7) .... (not / export) because this country buys everything we produce. It's very important to keep our factory clean and hygienic so everything (8) .... (wash) very carefully every night. Of course nobody (9) .... (allow) to smoke anywhere in the factory. Now I think lunch (10) .... (serve) in the canteen at the moment, so shall we go?

55 First, look at picture 1. Then, look at picture 2. Write what has been done and what hasn't. Four things are different and three things are the same. Use the verbs in the box.

| wash | close | ~~finish~~ | repair | turn off | turn off | ~~throw away~~ |

1   **2**

1 The flowers have been thrown away.
2 The letter hasn't been finished.
3 ....
4 ....
5 ....
6 ....
7 ....

56 Put the verb in brackets ( ) in the correct form, active or passive.

Here is the local news for Friday, February 14th.
Last night in Cowford many trees (1) *were blown* (blow) down in the storm. One tree (2) *fell* (fall) across the main road into Cowford. It (3) .... (take) away by the fire service during the night. Heavy rain also (4) .... (cause) problems on the roads. Some roads (5) .... (cover) by half a metre of water. Many motorists (6) .... (leave) their cars and (7) .... (walk) home. Now over to our reporter, Carol Black. Carol, what's happening?

Well, the situation this morning is better, and nearly back to normal. The last few cars (8) .... (remove) by the emergency services at the moment. And I can see the telephone engineers at work. The broken lines (9) .... (repair). The traffic (10) .... now .... (move) in and out of the town along the main roads.

Thank you Carol. And now one piece of good news.
Yesterday evening, a black BMW (11) .... (steal) from outside the home of Mr John Simpson. Mr Simpson (12) .... (telephone) the police. Later that evening, the car (13) .... (see) in the High Street by Mr Simpson's wife, Laura. It was outside the Red Lion Hotel. The keys were in the car, so she (14) .... (drive) it home! The police (15) .... (look) for a careless thief!

And finally, some football news.

We (16) .... just .... (hear) that Cowford Town are champions for the fourth time! A few minutes ago the referee (17) .... (blow) the whistle at the end of the game against Grimeton. Our reporter at the match, Kevin Anderson, (18) .... (wait) to talk to us at the stadium.

STUDIO: Kevin, (19) .... (be) it a good game?

KEVIN: Yes, excellent, very fast but unfortunately a bit rough.
Cowford's star player, Tony Ancock (20) .... (send) off because he (21) .... (kick) one of the Grimeton players. And the Grimeton goalkeeper (22) .... (hurt) when he (23) .... (crash) into one of the goalposts. He (24) .... (take) off the field with leg injuries, so both teams (25) .... (play) with ten men for the last few minutes.

STUDIO: Is he all right?

KEVIN: Well, we don't know. He (26) .... (take) to hospital at this moment. The manager (27) .... (think) it's serious.

STUDIO: Oh dear. That's a bad end to the match for Grimeton. What (28) .... (happen) now in the stadium?

KEVIN: The Cowford players (29) .... (walk) up the steps to receive the Champions Cup. And now back to the studio.

be/have/do and regular/irregular verbs   Units 23–24

57 Complete the sentences using the verbs in the box.

| has | weren't | is | haven't | didn't | doesn't | are | was | ~~am~~ | were |

1 I _am_ starting university in the autumn.
2 Frank isn't at work at the moment. He .... gone to Switzerland for a conference.
3 The Channel Tunnel .... built between 1985 and 1994.
4 Phillip .... eat meat. He's a vegetarian.
5 We .... been to Toronto before. This is our first time in Canada.
6 Look! Our cat .... playing with the dog from next door!
7 Your jeans .... washed last week and now they're dirty again!
8 I turned the stereo off because you .... listening to it.
9 A lot of leather shoes .... imported from Italy.
10 I .... go out last night.

58   Write the questions. Use **were you**, **did they**, **has he**, etc.

1 JEAN: When _were you_ born?
   FRED: May 29th, 1964.

2 STEVE: .... need an umbrella?
   JULIA: No, it isn't raining at the moment.

3 DENISE: .... coming to Jane's party tomorrow?
   HAZEL: Yes, I think so.

4 MIKE: I must go to the shops. What time .... close?
   CAROL: At 5.30.

5 ADAM: .... read John Presley's new book yet?
   MARY: No, I haven't. Is it good?

6 VAL: When .... get married?
   LIZ: A long time ago. When I was 21.

7 ED: I'm really sorry your car has gone. When .... stolen?
   FRANK: Yesterday. It was parked in the street outside my house.

8 LYNN: .... been in hospital before?
   LISA: No, this is her first time, and she's a bit worried.

9 MARK: .... waiting for a bus when I saw you last night?
   SARAH: No, a taxi.

59   Put the verb in brackets ( ) into the right form. Use the past simple (e.g. **sold**, **broke**, etc.) and past participle (e.g. **rung**, **gone**, etc.).

1 Sue _sold_ her motorbike when she _broke_ her leg last year. (sell / break)

2 I've _rung_ the doorbell three times and there's no answer. I think they've _gone_ out. (ring / go)

3 I .... the letter to Ruth but she .... to post it. (give / forget)

4 Ian hasn't .... his keys yet. He can't remember where he .... them. (find / leave)

5 Do you remember the photograph of Don that you .... me? Was it .... by a professional photographer? (show / take)

6 A lion .... from the national zoo yesterday but it was .... a few hours later. (escape / catch)

7 James has often .... about flying in a helicopter but he hasn't .... it yet. (think / do)

8 When she was younger, Paula always .... a ring which was .... to her by her grandmother. (wear / give)

9 Alan .... to swim when he was a baby. But he .... into a river when he was four years old and he has never .... again. (learn / fall / swim)

10 Jill .... ill last night so she .... to bed and .... for ten hours. (feel / go / sleep)

11 When I was younger, a teacher at my school .... me. It .... a lot and I have never .... it. (hit / hurt / forget)

I used to …

60 Complete the sentences. Use **used to** and a suitable verb.

George Medley is listening to a guide telling a group of visitors about the town of Stampford. He is thinking about Stampford in the past.

GEORGE
MEDLEY

GUIDE:
Stampford is a very busy town nowadays. There are lots of things to do.
For example, we have a big new cinema complex.
And this is the chemical factory. It's very important for the town. A lot of people work here.
Unfortunately, the river is not very clean now.
Broad Street is the main shopping street in town.
We now have a wonderful cheap bus service.
And of course, we've got lots of fast food restaurants.
And look, there's Paul Carr, our famous artist.
As you can see, Stampford is a good place to live.

GEORGE MEDLEY:
1 *It used to be* very quiet.

2 It .... a school.

3 I .... football in the park there.

4 I .... in that river.

5 Our family .... at number 23.
6 Everyone .... to the shops.
7 We .... at home.

8 He .... a waiter.

9 It .... better.

☺ Can you think of four things that you **used to do** when you were younger that you don't do now? You can use the following verbs to help you: live / play / speak / go / like / listen.

10 ....
11 ....
12 ....
13 ....

61 Read the text about the Inuit people of North America and complete it with the verbs below.
Use **used to** or the present simple (e.g. **he lives**, **they have**, etc.).

have	drive	wear	wear	live	take off	be
cook	~~call~~	hunt	go	take	hate	spend

IGLOO

SEAL

SNOWSHOES

FUR

The lives of the Inuit people of North America have changed a lot in 30 years.
First, their name: people (1) .used to call. them Eskimos, but now they are called Inuits, which means 'the people'.

They (2) .... in igloos in the winter but today, many of them live in houses in small towns. They (3) .... seals – they ate the meat and made clothes from the fur. Many of the people still (4) .... seal-skin clothes today because they are very warm. Remember, the weather is extremely cold for many months of the year. 85-year-old Inuit, Mariano Tagalik, told us a little about her early life.

'Our winter igloos were very warm. We (5) .... inside so sometimes it got too hot. When I was a child I (6) .... most of my clothes when I was in our igloo. In the short summers we lived in seal-skin tents, but I (7) .... as much time as possible playing outside.'

To move over the snow, they (8) .... special snowshoes on their feet, but today many Inuits (9) .... snowmobiles. These machines can travel long distances in a short time. In the past it (10) .... them days or weeks to travel the same distance.

Inuit children never (11) .... to school – they learnt everything from their parents but now, like all North Americans, they (12) .... about 10 years of school education.

Life is not as hard as it (13) ...., but many of the older Inuits (14) .... town life and want to go back to the old days.

What are you doing tomorrow?

62 Complete the conversation. Use the present continuous (e.g. **he's coming**) or the present simple (e.g. **he comes**).

Josie Turner is the export manager of a large international company. Harry Brentwood is a customer from Canada. They are trying to arrange an appointment for next week.

JOSIE: Hello, Josie Turner speaking.

HARRY: Oh Josie, this is Harry Brentwood. How are you? I (1) _'m coming_ (come) to London on Sunday and I'd like to meet you next week. Can we arrange a time?

JOSIE: I'd love to. When are you free?

HARRY: Well how about lunch on Monday?

JOSIE: I can't, I'm afraid. I (2) .... (have) lunch with our new Chairman. Tuesday at 10.30?

HARRY: No, no good. Dennis, my London agent, (3) .... (come) to the office. Wednesday afternoon is a possibility.

JOSIE: Not for me. My secretary, Jenny, (4) .... (get married) and all of us (5) .... (go) to the wedding. And on Thursday morning I (6) .... (drive) up to Manchester for a meeting with Bill Syms.

HARRY: What time (7) .... the meeting .... (start)?

JOSIE: 11.30 a.m. I've got an idea! Why don't you come with me? We can talk on the way.

HARRY: That sounds good. Oh, but wait a minute, I can't. I (8) .... (talk) to a group of business people about Canadian business opportunities at lunchtime.

JOSIE: So Friday, then.

HARRY: Yes. That's the only possibility because my return flight to Montreal (9) .... (leave) at 9.00 a.m. on Saturday. So, 11.30 a.m. on Friday morning at your office?

JOSIE: Yes, that's perfect. I'm really looking forward to seeing you then.

☺ Some friends of yours invite you to different things next week but you can't go to any of them because you're busy. Write what you are doing at those times. Use the present continuous (e.g. **I'm having**).

10 A: There's a party at my house on Tuesday night. Would you like to come?
   B: I can't, I'm afraid. _I'm having dinner with Mary._

11 A: Meet me on Wednesday evening in the city centre.
   B: I can't ....

12 A: See you on Friday at 12.30 p.m. outside the museum. OK?
   B: I can't ....

13 A: Jim wants you to come to the cinema with us on Saturday afternoon.
   B: I can't ....

14 A: Let's go for a walk on Sunday.
   B: I can't ....

63 Use the words below to write complete sentences or questions. Use the present continuous or the present simple.

1 A: Let's meet outside the cinema.
   B: What time / the film / start?
     What time does the film start?
   A: At 7.15 p.m.

2 A: What time / you / go / on Friday?
     What time are you going on Friday?
   B: After lunch.

3 A: Hurry up! We're late. The next bus / leave / in five minutes.

   B: OK, I'm ready.

4 A: Where / you / go / at the weekend?

                                           ?
   B: I don't know yet.

5 A: Let's get a taxi home after the concert.
   B: Why? It / not / finish late.

6 A: Jane / work at Brown's Restaurant tonight so she can't come to the party.

   B: Oh, that's a pity.

7 A: Why's Frank in bed so early tonight?
   B: He / leave / for France at 5 a.m. tomorrow.

8 A: Where / the next train / go to?

                                           ?
   B: Bristol, I think.

I'm going to ...   **Unit 27**

64 Write questions with **... going to ...** .

1 BEN: what / Dad / do?   *What's Dad going to do?*
   MUM: Paint the kitchen walls.
   BEN: what colour / he / do them?   *What colour's he going to do them?*
   MUM: White.

2 JILL: what / you / buy / for Paul's birthday? ....?
  MEG: I don't know yet.
  JILL: he / have / a party? ....?
  MEG: Yes, on Saturday.
3 TOM: you / buy / a new computer? ....?
  SUE: Yes.
  TOM: what kind / you / get? ....?
  SUE: An Apple Mac, I think.
4 MARY: what / Sarah / do / after university? ....?
  JACK: First, she's going to travel.
  MARY: how long / she / be away? ....?
  JACK: About six months.
5 PAUL: Joe and Kate / get married? ....?
  SALLY: Yes, in the autumn.
  PAUL: where / they / live? ....?
  SALLY: With her parents.

65 Write sentences using ... **going to** (**be**) ...

1 It's only 7 o'clock in the morning but the sun is shining and it's warm.
  It's going to be a beautiful day.
2 John is driving on the wrong side of the road! .... an accident!
3 Carol is eating her third box of chocolates! .... sick!
4 What a fantastic race! Roger is nearly there! Only 50 metres to the finish.
  .... win!
5 Look at those boys on that big bicycle! They're not safe. .... fall off!
6 This film is making me feel very sad. .... cry.

will/shall

66 Read what George says about his life at the moment and his future.

> **Friday 25th**
> At the moment I have to work very hard. I study at home every night and tonight is the same. I'll be at home as usual. I'll be in my bedroom with my books.
> But tomorrow is Saturday – no college and no work! So tomorrow morning I'll probably be in the city centre. I want to buy some clothes.
> College finishes next month so at the end of the month I'll be on holiday in Paris with my friends.
> A few years from now I'll probably be married.
> In 2010 I'll be 40 years old. My children will probably be at school.
> I don't know where I'll be in 2020.

Are these statements true? Correct the sentences that are wrong. Use **will** and **won't**.

1 George'll be at the cinema this evening. _No, he won't. He'll be at home._
2 He'll be in his bedroom. _True_
3 Tomorrow morning he'll be at college. ....
4 Next month he'll be in Paris. ....
5 He'll be on his own. ....
6 A few years from now, he'll probably be married. ....
7 He'll be 28 in 2001. ....
8 His children will probably be at university. ....
9 He'll be in Paris in 2020. ....

☺ And you? Where will you be? Write sentences about yourself. Use **I'll be ... / I'll probably be ... / I don't know where I'll be**.

This evening ....
Tomorrow morning ....
Next month ....
A few years from now ....
In 2010 ....

67 Complete the sentences. Use **will** ('ll) or **won't** + a verb from the box.

see	tell	~~win~~	stay	get

1 JANE: I'm going to the big baseball match tonight. My team, Dallas Cowboys, are playing.
  BEN: Do you think they *'ll win?*
  JANE: Of course. They're the best!

2 KATH: The new man in the sales department doesn't look very happy.
  LUCY: No, I don't think he .... very long.

3 PAT: Don't say anything to John about the surprise party on Saturday.
  SUE: Don't worry. I .... him.

4 FRED: You look sad. What's the matter?
  ZOE: My grandparents are on their way to Australia. They're going to live there, so I
         probably .... again.
  FRED: Why not? You can go there for a holiday.

5 SAM: Tony and Maria have known each other for a long time.
  TINA: Yes. I think they .... married soon.
  SAM: I don't think so. They haven't got any money.

68 Your grandmother has a few problems.
Offer to help her.
Write sentences with **Shall I ...?**

My eyes are not good. I can't read Jane's letter.
I'm thirsty.
It's a bit cold in here.
I can't open this packet of biscuits.
I can't hear what that man on TV is saying.
The dog needs some exercise.
I think the kitchen floor is dirty.

1 *Shall I read* it to you?
2 .... you a cup of tea?
3 .... the window?
4 .... it for you?
5 .... it up?
6 .... him for a walk?
7 .... it for you?

69 Joe and Phil went camping in Portugal last year. Now they are planning their next holiday. Write questions with **Shall we ...?** Look at the answers first.

JOE: It's time to start planning this summer's holiday. Where (1) *shall we go?*
PHIL: Let's go to Portugal again. I enjoyed it last year.
JOE: (2) .... in the same hotel?
PHIL: No, let's try something different. How about camping?
JOE: Great! I bought a new tent last year. (3) .... that?
PHIL: Yes, let's. (4) .... or fly?
JOE: Oh, drive I think because we'll have a lot of luggage.
PHIL: When (5) ....?
JOE: The middle of July is best for me. How about you?
PHIL: July is fine for me, too. (6) .... Tony to come with us?
JOE: No. The tent is only big enough for two people!

Review (future)

70 Put the verb in the present continuous (e.g. **they're going**) or the present simple (e.g. **I see**).

1 I usually ..*see*... (see) my parents at the weekend but this weekend I can't because they
..*are going*... (go) to London.

2 Julian .... (have) a holiday later this year. Normally he
.... (go) on holiday in July, but this year he can't.

3 Sue .... (not / often / stay) at home in the evenings but tonight she
.... (stay) in because there's an important football match on TV.

4 .... (you / take) your exam next month? .... (you / want)
to borrow my notes?

5 I .... (cook) the meals this weekend. Normally, Jane .... (do)
it but she's away all weekend.

71 What do you say in the following situations? Use **will** or the present continuous.

1 Jane tells you she cannot play tennis tonight because her partner is ill.
You offer to play with her. What do you say? .*I'll play with you.*...

2 Your young brother breaks his favourite toy train. He's very sad. You offer to buy him another
one. What do you say? ....

3 You and your sister have arranged to go shopping tomorrow. A friend invites you to lunch.
What do you say? I can't come ....

4 You're flying to Athens this afternoon. Your mother wants to know that you have arrived
safely. You offer to telephone her this evening. What do you say?

....

5 Your brother, Tony, and his wife, Rachel, come to dinner once a week at your house. Tonight
is the night. What do you say to your mother?
Don't forget that ....

6 Frank wants to go to the cinema to see 'Black Nights'. It's a horror film and you know he
doesn't like horror films. What do you say to him?
I don't think ....

7 Julia wants to know about your weekend plans. What does she ask you?
.... at the weekend?

8 Your plan is to stay at home all weekend. What do you say to Julia?
.... all weekend.

72 Are the underlined words right or wrong? Correct the sentences that are wrong.

1 The new road <u>shall</u> be open in the summer.   *The road will be open in the summer.*
2 The exam <u>starts</u> at 8.30 tomorrow.   *right*
3 I've got my ticket. I <u>will go</u> to Spain. ....
4 You look tired. Sit down. I'm <u>making</u> you a cup of coffee. ....
5 What time <u>is</u> the sun <u>rising</u> tomorrow? ....
6 Where <u>do you go</u> for lunch today? ....
7 <u>Shall we learn</u> Spanish next year? ....
8 Do you think it <u>is raining</u> later? ....
9 I can't come because <u>I'll be</u> on holiday. ....

10 (*on the phone*) It's Ann you want to speak to. Just one minute, please. <u>I'm going to call</u> her.

11 Don't worry about me, Mum. <u>I'll write</u> to you every day from the States.

73 Write complete sentences.

1 **present continuous or will?**
JANE: What did Jack say on the phone?
ANNE: He / have / a party on Saturday.
    He's having a party on Saturday.
JANE: you / go? *Are you going?*
ANNE: Yes. I like Jack's parties.
JANE: Did he invite me, too?
ANNE: Yes, but you can't come, can you?
JANE: No, I / be / away at the weekend.
    No, I'll be away at the weekend.

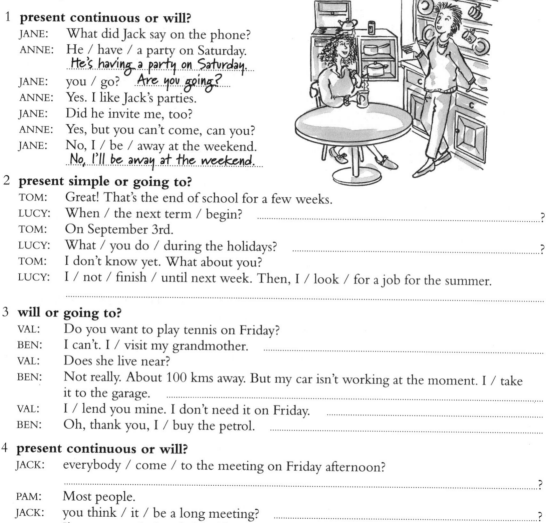

2 **present simple or going to?**
TOM: Great! That's the end of school for a few weeks.
LUCY: When / the next term / begin? .... ?
TOM: On September 3rd.
LUCY: What / you do / during the holidays? .... ?
TOM: I don't know yet. What about you?
LUCY: I / not / finish / until next week. Then, I / look / for a job for the summer.

3 **will or going to?**
VAL: Do you want to play tennis on Friday?
BEN: I can't. I / visit my grandmother. ....
VAL: Does she live near?
BEN: Not really. About 100 kms away. But my car isn't working at the moment. I / take it to the garage. ....
VAL: I / lend you mine. I don't need it on Friday. ....
BEN: Oh, thank you, I / buy the petrol. ....

4 **present continuous or will?**
JACK: everybody / come / to the meeting on Friday afternoon?
.... ?
PAM: Most people.
JACK: you think / it / be a long meeting? .... ?
PAM: I'm not sure. It / probably / be about 3 hours. Why?

JACK: I / go to the dentist at 5.30. I made the appointment two weeks ago.

might

74   A friend is asking you about some plans. You're not sure. Use **might** (**not**).

1   A: Where are you going this weekend?
    B: I don't know yet. _I might go to Tim's party_ (Tim's party)
        but _I might not go anywhere_ (not / anywhere).

2   A: It's a national holiday tomorrow so there's no public transport. How are Jane and Sue
        going to get there?
    B: I don't know. It'll be difficult. They .... (taxi)
        but .... (not / come).

3   A: Who are you going to invite to dinner?
    B: I haven't decided yet. .... (Sarah)
        but .... (not / Tony).

4   A: What new clothes does Clare want to buy on Saturday?
    B: She's not sure yet. .... (some jeans)
        but .... (not / anything).

☺   What about you? What are you going to do this weekend? Use **might** (**not**) in your answers.

5   _I might go to the cinema._   7   ....
6   8   ....

75   Read this information about Peter's holiday. Write sentences with (**not**) **going to** and **might** (**not**).

Peter's going on holiday tomorrow. He's packed his suitcases and he's ready to leave early in the morning. He's going to China. It's going to be a busy holiday because there are a lot of things he wants to do and see, and some things he hasn't decided about yet.

sure	**perhaps**
1 Visit the Forbidden City, Beijing	2 Not have time to visit the museums
3 Walk along The Great Wall	4 Try the rice wine
5 Not eat western food	6 Go on a boat trip
7 Learn a few phrases of Chinese	8 Not come home!

1   _Peter is going to visit the Forbidden City in Beijing._
2   _He might not have time to visit the museums._
3   ....
4   ....
5   ....
6   ....
7   ....
8   ....

can and could

76 Paula has got a problem. Use **can** or **can't** + the verb in brackets ( ).

Oh dear! Where's my key? I (1) *can't find* (find) it. Oh look! It's on the kitchen table. I
(2) .... (see) it. Now what am I going to do? I (3) .... (get) in. I
(4) .... (climb) the tree to the window on the first floor. It's too high. I
(5) .... (telephone) for help because I haven't got my money with me. Hey, what's
that noise in the sitting room? I (6) .... (hear) something. Oh good, it's Peter. He's
at home. I'm safe!

The next day, Peter tells his friend, Kate, about Paula's problem.
7 Paula *couldn't find* her key yesterday.
8 She .... it on the kitchen table.
9 She .... in.
10 She .... the tree.
11 She .... for help.
12 She .... someone in the sitting room – it was me!

77 Complete these sentences. Use **can't** or **couldn't** + a verb from the box.

type	see	speak	~~find~~	come
catch	~~sleep~~	answer	understand	

1 I'd like to read Jim's letter. The only problem is I *can't find* my glasses.
2 Kevin was really tired last night but he *couldn't sleep.*
3 Jane would like to work in an office, but unfortunately she ....
4 People said he was a very interesting speaker, but I .... him.
5 Sue didn't pass her Maths exam because she .... the questions.
6 I've got two tickets for the ballet on Saturday, but unfortunately Frank
....
7 Maria's dog ran out of the house and she .... it.
8 A: I'd like to live in Paris. B: Me too, but I .... French very well.
9 (*at the cinema*) Those people in front of me are very tall. I .... the screen.

45

78 You are staying in a hotel. What do you say in these situations? Use **Can / Could you …?** or **Can / Could I …?**

1 You want the receptionist to turn the air-conditioning off in your room because you're cold.
   Could you (or Can you) turn the air-conditioning off, please?

2 There is only one towel in your room. You want another one.
   Can I (or Could I) have another towel, please?

3 You want the receptionist to give you a wake-up call at 6.30 in the morning.
   ....?

4 You want breakfast in your room tomorrow morning.
   ....?

5 You want to leave your passport and travellers cheques in the hotel safe.
   ....?

6 There is no hair dryer in your room. You want to borrow one.
   ....?

7 You want the receptionist to get a taxi for you.
   ....?

must/mustn't/needn't Unit 32

79 Complete each sentence. Use **must / mustn't / had to** + a verb.

1 Jill and Terry will be home from school soon. I *must cook* their lunch.
2 Derek .... late at the office last night. There was an important job to do.
3 If you are absent for more than three days, you .... a letter from your doctor.
4 The dentist has told Alan he .... any more sweet things. His teeth are in bad condition.
5 When Barbara was five years old, she .... to school, but she didn't want to.
6 Let's catch an earlier train tomorrow. We .... late for the meeting.
7 My hair feels really dirty. I .... it tonight.
8 I forgot my front door key yesterday so I .... into the house through a window.

80 Complete the sentences. Use **mustn't** or **needn't** + a verb from the box. Use each verb twice.

~~help~~   ask   read   leave   work

1 Carol *mustn't help* you with your homework. It's important that you do it yourself.
2 You *needn't help* with the shopping. John has already done it.
3 We .... Bill about his holiday. He doesn't want to talk about it.
4 I just want a general idea of the story so I .... all the book.
5 You .... Harry for the answer. I can tell you.
6 You look really tired. You studied all night last night, so tonight you .... so hard.
7 You .... yet! You haven't had anything to eat.
8 You .... my letters. They're private.
9 We .... yet. We've got plenty of time to get to the station.
10 I'm sure the shop won't be busy so you .... if you don't want to.

should

81 Make one sentence with **should** and one sentence with **shouldn't**.

1 GARY: I always feel tired these days. What do you think I should do?
  ANNE: *You should have* a holiday. *You shouldn't work* so hard.
2 GARY: I've got another hole in one of my teeth. What do you think I should do?
  ANNE: .... to the dentist. .... so many sweets.
3 GARY: I've got a terrible headache again. What do you think I should do?
  ANNE: .... an aspirin. .... without your glasses.
4 GARY: I've got a bad cough. What do you think I should do?
  ANNE: .... some medicine. .... so many cigarettes.
5 GARY: Bill wants to borrow my car for the weekend, but he's a terrible driver. What do you think I should do?
  ANNE: .... him that you need it. .... it to him.

82 You are asking a friend for advice. Make questions with **Do you think I / we should …?**

1 There are two buttons missing on this shirt I've just bought.
  Do you think I should take it back to the shop?
2 I think I work very hard but I don't get a big salary.
  .... my boss for more money?
3 Simon's late again, and the train leaves in five minutes.
  .... a bit longer or go without him?
4 Martina has been sleeping for 18 hours and it's lunchtime soon.
  .... her up?
5 Jane is very nervous about going on holiday alone.
  .... with her?
6 We must be at the airport at 6.00 a.m. and the buses are not very good in the mornings.
  .... a taxi?
7 Burnt toast again! This toaster is getting worse.
  .... a new one?

83 What advice would you give in the following situations? Use **should**.

1   Alan had a terrible quarrel with his wife at the weekend. It was his fault.
    What do you think he should do? I think _he should apologise to his wife._

2   Jane watches videos every night. She never goes out with her friends.
    What advice do you give? I think ....

3   David and Paula haven't got much money. But they go out every night and spend money. At
    the end of the month they can't pay their gas and electricity bills. What advice would you
    give? I don't think ....

4   Joseph is very intelligent, but he wants to leave school and get a job. His parents think he
    ought to go to university. What do you think?
    I think ....

5   Maria told me some interesting news last night, but she said, 'Please don't tell anyone.' Now
    Clare has asked me about Maria's news. What do you think I should do?
    I don't think ....

I have to

84 Write questions using **... have to ...** Look at the answers before you write the questions. Some of the
questions are in the present and some of them are in the past.

1   JOE: At school, I had to learn a lot of irregular verbs by heart. What
             did you have to learn by heart?
    CATH: The dates of all the kings and queens in history. It was boring!

2   JEAN: I really must go home. I have to get up early tomorrow.
    LIZ: What about Chris? .... early tomorrow?
    JEAN: No, he doesn't, so he can stay a bit longer.

3   BRIAN: I didn't pass my driving test first time. I had to take it three times. How many times
             .... your driving test?
    TOM: Only once. I passed first time.

4   PHIL: This book is so boring. I hope I finish reading it soon.
    CAROL: Why .... it?
    PHIL: Because I've got a literature exam next week.

5   NED: My mother wanted me to be a pianist. So for years I had to go to music lessons.
    DIANA: What about your sister? .... to music lessons, too?
    NED: No, she had to do ballet lessons.

6   SUE: I must be at work early tomorrow. I arrived at 10 o'clock this morning.
    MEG: What time .... there normally?
    SUE: 8.30!

85 Complete the sentences with the correct form of **have to**. Some of them are in the present and some of them are in the past. Use the verb in brackets ( ).

1 MARK: I don't like cabbage.
  SUE: That's OK. You can leave it. You _don't have to eat it._ (eat)

2 DAVE: We have to write a 1000-word essay before next Friday.
  JILL: What about me? _____ one, too? (write)
  DAVE: Yes, I think so. Everybody has to do one.

3 PAUL: John's going to the bank later. He needs some money.
  MICK: He _____ to the bank. I can lend him some. (go)

4 ANN: CAN YOU PASS ME THE SALT, PLEASE?
  PETE: You _____ I'm not deaf! (shout)

5 PAT: Did Ruth enjoy her summer job in France?
  SAM: No, she hated it. She _____ every day, so she wasn't able to see anything of the country. (work)

6 JOHN: Which job is Harry going to accept?
  RUTH: I don't know. He's going to think about it at the weekend. He _____ today. (decide)

7 IAN: I really enjoyed Jane's party last night, but there were no buses home after midnight.
  LYNN: _____ home? (walk)
  IAN: Yes, and it was a long way!

8 BETH: What's the matter with Tim?
  KATE: I'm not sure. The doctor says he _____ in bed for a few days. (stay)

9 JOE: Was Tina angry when you told her the news?
  FRED: She already knew it so I _____ her. (tell)

there ... and it ...   Units 36–38

86 Put in **there** or **it**.

1 MUM: _There's_ a good programme on TV tonight. _It's_ about computers.
  DAD: I'm not interested in computers. Is _____ a long programme?
  MUM: No, only half an hour. Why?
  DAD: Because _____'s another programme I want to watch at 9.30.

2 JUAN: Excuse me. Is _____ a bank near here?
  MARK: Yes, _____'s one on the corner of Broad Street.
  JUAN: Is _____ open at lunchtime?
  MARK: Yes, I think so.

3 JANE: (standing outside a restaurant) This is the new Mexican restaurant.
  MARY: Is _____ expensive?
  JANE: No, I don't think so. Look, _____'s an empty table. Let's go in.

4 DAVE: Mum, _____ isn't any soap in the bathroom.
  MUM: Yes, _____ is. _____'s a new packet on the shelf.
  DAVE: I can't see _____.
  MUM: _____'s next to the shampoo.

87 You are on a tour of the National Museum. You're looking at paintings. Put in **there is / are / was / were / has been / will be**.

Welcome to the National Museum, ladies and gentlemen. We've only got one hour and
(1) _there is_ a lot to see, so let's start.
On your left, you can see a painting by Rembrandt. (2) .... seven works by
Rembrandt here now. Last year (3) .... eight but sadly (4) .... a
robbery at the museum some months ago and the painting was stolen.
For those of you who are interested, (5) .... a major exhibition of Rembrandt's
work in London at the moment, and one next year in Amsterdam. I'm sure (6) ....
a lot of visitors to both exhibitions.
Now in this room, (7) .... a very famous painting by Picasso. And this painting on
the right is very interesting. It's by an Italian artist but we don't know which one. Oh no! It's
disappeared. (8) .... another robbery! Quick! Phone the police!

88 Put in **it/there + is(n't)/was(n't)**.

We had some interesting weather in the country yesterday. In Brightlea, (1) _there was_ snow.
(2) .... unusual to have snow in the spring in this country. But last winter, when
everybody wanted to go skiing, (3) .... any snow at all.
Here in Wellbrough, the capital city, (4) .... windy yesterday. But that's normal.
(5) .... often a strong wind in spring. But (6) .... also very cold.
My sister lives in Stratton, on the east side of the country and she said that yesterday
(7) .... really dark in the middle of the afternoon and (8) .... a storm. It
frightened her children.
And today, (9) .... cloudy. (10) .... raining yet but I think it will soon.

Ask Martin questions about the weather in the town where he lives. Use **it** or **there**.

		YOU:	MARTIN:
11	(a lot of rain in spring?)	_Is there a lot of rain in spring?_	Yes, quite a lot.
12	(raining / at the moment?)	....?	No.
13	(sunny / at the moment?)	....?	Yes.
14	(any snow in winter?)	....?	Sometimes.
15	(any snow / last winter?)	....?	Yes, quite a lot.

I do / Have you? / So am I etc.
(auxiliary verbs)

89 Use the information about Simon and David to complete the sentences. Begin each sentence with **'Simon …'**.

		SIMON:	DAVID:
1	Have you got a car?	no	yes
2	Are you interested in sport?	yes	no
3	Do you live in a town?	yes	no
4	Are you married?	no	yes
5	Have you got any brothers and sisters?	yes	no
6	Were you good at school?	yes	no
7	Did you study at university?	no	yes
8	Are you going on holiday this year?	yes	no
9	Have you visited many countries?	no	yes

1 Simon _hasn't got a car but David has._
2 Simon _is interested in sport but David isn't._
3 Simon ....
4 ....
5 ....
6 ....
7 ....
8 ....
9 ....

90 Write answers. Use **Do you?**, **Isn't it?**, etc.

1 I fell off my bike yesterday.	_Did you?_	Are you all right now?
2 I don't want to meet Jim.	.........................?	Why not?
3 My husband can't cook at all.	.........................?	What a pity.
4 Jane has lent me her laptop for tonight.	.........................?	That's good of her.
5 You forgot to telephone me yesterday.	.........................?	I'm sorry.
6 David doesn't use his car very much.	.........................?	How does he get to work?
7 It hasn't rained for over two weeks.	.........................?	That's very unusual.
8 I'm not going to eat chocolate anymore.	.........................?	Are you on a diet?
9 I was ill yesterday.	.........................?	What was the matter?
10 Your answer was wrong, I'm afraid.	.........................?	What was the right answer?

91 Complete these sentences with a positive question tag (**is it?**, **can you?**, etc.) or a negative question tag (**weren't you?**, **hasn't it?**, etc.)

A: Now, you were born in Alaska, (1) *weren't you?*
B: Yes, that's right.
A: And then you all moved to New York, (2) ....?
B: Well, no. We moved to Los Angeles first, then to New York.
A: Sorry. But you don't live in New York now, (3) ....?
B: No, my family do, but I live in Washington.
A: I see. Now, you've got two brothers, (4) ....? And you are all actors. That's very unusual, (5) ....?
B: Yes, I think it is, but my parents were both actors, so …
A: They weren't very happy at first about you becoming an actor, (6) ....?
B: No, not at first. They didn't want me to follow in their footsteps. But now they're really pleased about my success.
A: I know you've acted with your brothers in a film but you haven't made a film with your parents yet, (7) ....?
B: No, but we are hoping to do one together next year.
A: That's very interesting. Tell me about it.
B: Well, it's about …

92 Mark has the same kind of job as Sandra. Write what Mark says. Use **too** or **either**.

SANDRA
1 I work in a hotel.
2 I can't speak a foreign language.
3 My manager is very good.
4 I haven't got any friends at work.
5 I don't work at the weekends.
6 I started work last year.
7 I'm bored with my job.
8 My salary isn't very good.

MARK
I do too.
I can't either.
Mine ...

isn't/haven't/don't etc. (negatives)

Unit 42

93 Read this information about John and Mary. Use **So ... Mary** (e.g. **So does Mary.**), **Neither ... Mary** (e.g. **Neither can Mary.**) or **Mary ...** (e.g. **Mary wouldn't.**).

JOHN		MARY		
likes comedy films		same	1	*So does Mary.*
would love to go to America		different	2	*Mary wouldn't.*
can't play tennis very well		same	3	*Neither*
isn't married		same	4	
doesn't like jazz music very much		different	5	
hasn't got any brothers		same	6	
is looking for a new job		different	7	
went to university		same	8	
never goes to discos		same	9	
will be 22 next birthday		same	10	

☺ And you? Write true answers about yourself where you are the same as Mary or John. Use **so ... I** or **neither ... I.**

Mary likes comedy films and so do I.
John can't play tennis very well and neither can I.

....
....
....

isn't/haven't/don't etc. (negatives)

94 Complete these sentences with a verb in the negative form.

1 William and Eve *didn't go* (not / go) to the cinema last night.
2 I'm hungry. I .... (not / have) dinner yet.
3 Sarah .... (not / do) her shopping during the week. She always does it on Saturdays.
4 Please .... (not / watch me) when I'm cooking. I ....
   .... (not / like) it.
5 I .... (not / read) the newspaper at the moment. You can borrow it.
6 You .... (not / come) and see me yesterday.
7 These flowers .... (not / look) good on the table. Put them on the TV.
8 It .... (not / rain) at the moment. We can go out.
9 Let's take Sally to the Chinese restaurant. She .... (not / eat) Chinese food before.

95 Martha is listening to Madame Petra. She is talking about Martha and her life. Unfortunately, a lot of it is wrong.

> I think your name begins with an 'A', maybe Andrea or Angela. You were born in England but you lived in Germany when you were younger. You can speak four languages.
>
> You're married and you've got two children. Your husband is a scientist, I think. Your parents live in your house with you and your family.
>
> Your son's birthday is in June. He's a teenager and he will be 14 next June. You're going to buy him a new bicycle and a new camera for his birthday. You are very happy with your family and I think you would like to have two or more children.

Martha tells her where she is wrong. Complete her sentences with a verb in the negative form.

Martha says:
You're wrong about me.

1 My name _isn't Andrea._ It's Martha.
2 I .... in England. I was born in Scotland.
3 I .... in Germany when I was younger. I lived in the USA.
4 I .... four languages. I can only speak two.
5 Yes, I'm married but I .... two children. I've got one, Tony.
6 My husband .... a scientist. He's a salesman.
7 My parents .... in my house. They live in their own house.
8 You're right, my son's birthday *is* in June, but next June he .... 14, he'll be 10.
9 Yes, I'm going to buy him a new bicycle but I .... him a new camera.
10 I am very happy with my family but I .... to have any more children.

questions

96 You are asking Jack some questions. Write the full questions.

YOU   JACK

1	(live?) *Where do you live?*	In the middle of the town.
2	(do?) ....?	I'm a teacher.
3	(university?) ....?	Yes, I studied physics.
4	(married?) ....?	Yes, I am.
5	(meet / your wife?) ....?	At a wedding!
6	(any children?) ....?	Yes, a daughter called Emily.
7	(Emily / to school?) ....?	No, not yet. She's only three.
8	(your wife / work?) ....?	Yes, at home. She looks after Emily.
9	(enjoy your job?) ....?	Yes, most of the time.
10	(it / a difficult job?) ....?	Sometimes, but I like the children.
11	(weeks / holiday?) ....?	Twelve weeks a year.

97 Complete these subject and object questions. Use the verb in brackets ( ).

1 A: There are some beautiful flowers on the table.
  B: Who *put them* there? (put)

2 A: I went to the cinema last night.
  B: What *did you see?* (see)

3 A: Oh dear! I spent a lot of money yesterday.
  B: What ....? (buy)

4 A: We're all really hungry after our swim.
  B: OK. Who .... a sandwich? (want)

5 A: I'm going to explain to Meg why I can't see her again.
  B: What .... to her? (say)

6 A: Julia likes George but he doesn't really like her. Someone else does.
  B: Who .... Julia? (like)

7 A: I can hear music next door.
  B: Me too. Who .... the piano? (play)

8 A: ... and just at that moment, a man opened the window and started to climb out.
  B: What .... next? (happen)

9 A: Have you got a problem with the exercise, Maria?
  B: Yes. I don't understand this word. What ....? (mean)

98 Complete the questions. Each question ends with a preposition (**to/for/at/with**, etc.).

1 A: Jane's been talking on the telephone for hours.
  B: Who *'s she talking to?*

2 A: Jim has been waiting a long time.
  B: Who ....?

3 A: I wrote six letters yesterday.
  B: Who ....?

4 A: The new man in the Export Department is a Spanish speaker.
  B: Where ....?

5 A: Sarah doesn't live on her own. She shares her apartment.
  B: Who ....?

6 A: You really should read this book. It's a wonderful story.
  B: What ....?

7 A: Oxford is a very famous city.
  B: What ....?

8 A: We sold our car last week.
  B: Who ....?

9 A: Laura has been standing and looking out of the window for a long time.
  B: What ....?

99 Write questions with **which/what/how** + the word in brackets ( ).

1 A: We can catch the train if we hurry.
  B: *What time does it* leave?   (time)

2 A: I'm learning Spanish, French and Arabic at the moment.
  B: *Which language do you* prefer?   (language)

3 A: I'm really tired today. I went for a long walk yesterday.
  B: .... walk?   (far)

4 A: I've got dark hair but my sister's is completely different.
  B: .... her hair?   (colour)

5 A: Everyone thinks I'm younger than Tom because he's much taller than me.
  B: .... he?   (tall)

6 A: We must go. Are you ready?
  B: Nearly. .... wear – the black ones or the brown ones?   (shoes)

100 Find the mistakes and correct them.

1 What time leaves the train?   *What time does the train leave?*
2 Why you didn't ring me last night?   ....?
3 To who are you giving that present?   ....?
4 How much has spent Mary?   ....?
5 Where did Jenny went for her holidays last year?   ....?
6 What do you usually in the evenings?   ....?
7 What did happen next?   ....?
8 When was built the Taj Mahal?   ....?

101 Complete the questions. Sometimes there is more than one possible question.

1 REBECCA: *Did you* enjoy your holiday?
  DENISE: Yes thanks, it was wonderful.
  REBECCA: Where ....?
  DENISE: To Jamaica.
  REBECCA: Who ....?
  DENISE: Two friends from my office.
  REBECCA: What ....?
  DENISE: It was sunny every day.

2 ROBERT: What ....?
  DANIEL: I've broken my arm.
  ROBERT: How ....?
  DANIEL: I fell off my bike.
  ROBERT: .... hurt?
  DANIEL: Not now, but it did.

3 LINDA: What ....?
  CLARE: I'm a teacher.
  LINDA: .... in a primary or a secondary school?
  CLARE: Secondary. My pupils are aged 14 to 16.
  LINDA: What ....?
  CLARE: Maths and physics.
  LINDA: How long ....?
  CLARE: Since 1988.

Do you know where ...?

102 Answer these questions with **I don't know** + the word in brackets ( ).

1 Is it Sue's birthday next week?
  (when) *I don't know when it is.*

2 Is she leaving because she's unhappy?
  (why) ....

3 Are John and Julia getting married this summer?
  (when) ....

4 Is that your new camera? It looks expensive. Did it cost a lot?
  (how much) ....

5 Did *Ann* tell you the news about Frank?
  (who) ....

6 Did John buy you a watch for your last birthday?
  (what) ....

103   Write questions with **Do you know where/when/what …**, etc.

1   You want to know the time of the first train to London tomorrow morning. Ask the person in the information office.
  Do you know when the first train to London is tomorrow morning?

2   All the shops are closed today. You want to know why. Ask.
  ....?

3   You want to find the Regent Hotel. You ask a stranger in the street.
  ....?

4   Someone told you that John is going to leave his job. You want to know why.
  ....?

5   Someone told you that Mrs Smith, your old teacher, has died. You want to know when.
  ....?

104   Some words in this report are difficult to read. Ask questions to get the missing information. Use **Do you know …**

John Carter left home at (1) ▦▦▦▦▦ yesterday morning. He was wearing a (2) ▦▦▦▦▦ and a ▦▦▦▦▦ He wasn't alone. (3) ▦▦▦▦▦ was with him. First he went into a shop and bought a camera. It cost (4) ▦▦▦▦▦ Then he went into a (5) ▦▦▦▦▦ shop and came out carrying a long, thin package. The person with him was laughing, probably because (6) ▦▦▦▦▦ They walked to the station and caught the fast train which was going to (7) ▦▦▦▦▦ We know that journey usually takes (8) ▦▦▦▦▦ but yesterday it was much slower. My officers were at Dover station waiting for the two men but they were not on the train.

1   *Do you know what time he left home yesterday morning?*
2   ....
3   ....
4   ....
5   ....
6   ....
7   ....
8   ....

She said that … / He told me to … (reported speech)

105 Who is coming to the party on Saturday? Write sentences with **He/She said (that) …** or **He/She told me (that) …**

CAROLINE: I'm working really hard. I don't have time to go out in the evenings.

STEPHEN: I've got a few days' holiday. I'm going to Italy.

DAVE: I'm ill. I've been in bed for two days.

ANNA: I don't like parties. I can't dance.

SUE: I love parties. I'll be free on Saturday.

MARIA

TIM

MARIA: Did you invite Caroline to our party on Saturday?

TIM: Yes, but she can't come. She said (1) *she was working really hard* and (2) *she didn't have time to go out in the evenings.*

MARIA: OK. What about Stephen?

TIM: No. He said (3) .... and (4) ....

MARIA: Dave?

TIM: No. He said (5) .... and (6) ....

MARIA: Anna?

TIM: No, not Anna. She said (7) .... and (8) ....

MARIA: What about Sue?

TIM: Yes. She said (9) .... and (10) ....

MARIA: Good. That's a start!

106 Put in **say/said** or **tell/told**.

1 What did he _tell_ you to do?
2 Lena .... that the banks were closed on Saturdays.
3 Have you .... him your news?
4 I think she .... she couldn't come to the party.
5 Jackie .... to me that she wanted to see you.
6 I .... him not to speak on the phone for too long.
7 Did Sam .... anything about me?
8 I didn't .... the teacher why I was late.

107   At the office. Jane's manager is looking for her. Read what these people say about her.

Half an hour later.
MANAGER: Oh Jane. You're here. I asked everybody where you were.

1   Clare said *you were in the photocopy room.*
2   Paul said ....
3   Stuart said ....
4   ....
5   ....
6   ....
7   .... and ....

Where were you? (Finish with your own ideas!)
JANE: I was ....

---

do / to do / doing   **Units 50–53**

108   Choose the correct form of the verb.

1   Could I *borrow* your dictionary, please?
    to borrow / borrow / borrowing

2   I would like .... the President of our country.
    meet / meeting / to meet

3   Why is that car .... outside our house?
    stop / to stop / stopping

4   You don't look well. You should .... to bed.
    going / to go / go

5   Do we have .... now? I'm enjoying myself.
    to leave / leaving / leave

6   A: Shall I .... off the TV?   B: Yes, please.
    turn / turning / to turn

7   Harry was .... out of the window when he heard a loud noise.
    look / to look / looking

8   We used .... a dog but it died last year.
    having / to have / have

9   A: When are you going .... John the news? B: Tonight, I think.
    tell / telling / to tell

10 I must .... some postcards this weekend.
    to write / writing / write

11 Sally says she wants .... a nurse when she's older.
    being / to be / be

12 You didn't need .... any more eggs. We had some in the fridge.
    buy / to buy / buying

109   Put the verb in the right form, using **to ...** or **-ing**.

Dear Sally

Thank you for your last letter. It was good to hear from you. My big news is that
I've decided (1) ..to change.. (change) jobs. I finish (2) ..working.. (work) at Simpsons next
month and start in my new company, Galt, the week after. Simpsons didn't want me
(3) .... (leave) but Galt offered me more money and more opportunities. I
hope (4) .... (be) a manager there in two years.

   By the way, I forgot (5) .... (tell) you – I'm learning (6) ....
(drive). My new company offered (7) .... (let) me use one of their cars, which
was very good of them. I had a lot of problems at first because I wanted
(8) .... (do) everything quickly. My teacher thought I was a bit dangerous on
the road! He suggested (9) .... (slow) down, and now it's getting better.

   I'm having a party on the 25th and would love (10) .... (see) you.

   Perhaps you could persuade your brother (11) .... (come) with you as well.
I really enjoyed (12) .... (dance) with him at your party.

   My neighbours have promised (13) .... (go) out for the evening, so we can
play the music as loud as we want.

   I must stop (14) .... (write) now and do some work. See you on the 25th, I
hope.

   Love
      Claire

---

110 Complete sentences with **advised/persuaded/let** etc. Use **to** if necessary.

1 The doctor said I should stop eating chocolate.
The doctor *advised me to stop eating chocolate.* (advise)

2 I learnt to drive from my brother.
My brother .... (teach)

3 I said to David: 'Don't play with those matches.'
I .... (tell)

4 Stuart didn't allow his young sons to play with toy guns.
Stuart .... (let)

5 Jane didn't want to come swimming with us, but we asked her again and again and in the end she said, 'yes'.
We .... (persuade)

6 I was surprised that you married him.
I .... (expect)

7 My father said I had to pay back all the money I borrowed.
My father .... (make)

111 Finish each sentence with **(to) do something** or **(for) something**. Use your own ideas.

1 Tim went upstairs to *wash his hair.*
2 Jim went upstairs for *a book.*
3 I wrote to Mary to ....
4 Jane is going to ring the airport for ....
5 Let's open the window for ....
6 Mark turned on the TV to ....
7 Kevin is going to the kitchen ....
8 You need more money ....
9 Lucy hasn't got enough time ....
10 Jill waited a long time ....

112 Which ones are right? Sometimes only one sentence is right, sometimes two are right.

1 A: Why are you going to the post office?
   B: a) To get some stamps. *right*
      b) For getting some stamps. *wrong*
      c) For some stamps. *right*

2 a) Kate telephoned the station for asking about the London trains. ....
   b) Kate telephoned the station to ask about the London trains. ....
   c) Kate telephoned the station for information about the London trains. ....

3 a) I'm waiting for the rain stopping. ....
   b) I'm waiting for the rain to stop. ....
   c) I'm waiting for the rain stop. ....

4 a) We don't need much money to buy tickets. ....
   b) We don't need much money for tickets. ....
   c) We don't need much money for buy tickets. ....

Review (do / to do / doing)

113 Complete these sentences with the verbs from the box. Put them in the right form using **to ...** or **-ing**.

~~swim~~	ask	speak	meet	answer
learn	shop	look for	~~go~~	wait

1 Would you like *to go* to the new Thai restaurant for dinner?
2 Everybody enjoyed *swimming* in the lake.
3 My younger brother is interested in .... to play tennis.
4 Why did you take my dictionary without .... me?
5 Kathy's mother asked her not .... on the telephone for too long.
6 James flew to San Francisco .... his American cousins for the first time.
7 Mike left his village .... a job in the city.
8 Pam closed the door before .... the phone.
9 Peter wanted us .... for him outside the bank.
10 Let's go .... in the city centre. I need a new pair of jeans.

114 Complete the sentences. Put the verbs in brackets ( ) in the correct form.

JIM: What are you doing this weekend?
PAT: Well on Saturday we're going (1) *swimming* (swim). Would you like (2) *to come* (come)
       with us?
JIM: I can't swim without someone (3) .... (hold) me. I've been thinking of
       (4) .... (have) lessons.
PAT: Well, I can help you. I taught Clive (5) .... (swim).
JIM: Did you? OK, I'll come on Saturday.

BEN: Oh dear! I'm not very good at (6) .... (cook).
ALAN: What are you trying (7) .... (make)?
BEN: A cheese souffle.
ALAN: Let me (8) .... (help) you.
BEN: No, it's OK thanks. I must (9) .... (learn).

JANE: What did you do after (10) .... (finish) school?
ROB: I studied law. My father is a lawyer and he persuaded me (11) .... (go)
       to law school.
JANE: Did you enjoy it?
ROB: Not really, because it wasn't my choice. My father made me (12) .... (do)
       it. I wanted (13) .... (be) a journalist.
JANE: So what happened?
ROB: After two years of law school I left without (14) .... (tell) my father, and
       went (15) .... (live) in France.
JANE: And now you work for a French newspaper in London.
ROB: Yes, that's right.

I/me/my/mine/myself etc.

115 Complete the sentences. Use **I/she/they** etc. and **us/him/you** etc.

1 He likes Jane but ..*she doesn't like him.*.
2 We're looking at Mr and Mrs Warner but ....
3 She wants to talk to me but ....
4 Jo and Mary often write to you but ....
5 I want to meet him but ....
6 You can telephone us but ....
7 He visits his grandparents but ....

116 Put in **my/your/his/its** etc.

1 Did you enjoy ..*your*.. holiday?
2 I forgot .... umbrella this morning so I got wet.
3 When are we moving to .... new house?
4 The neighbours are angry because someone stole .... car last night.
5 Sydney is famous for .... opera house.
6 Oliver's got two sisters. .... older sister is married.
7 The lion lifted .... head and looked at us.
8 Jill had a wonderful time. It was the best holiday of .... life.
9 My husband gave me .... grandmother's ring when we got married.
10 I'm sorry I didn't telephone you. I lost .... number.

117 Complete the letter. Use **I/you/he** etc. or **her/him/them** etc. or **our/your/their** etc. or **mine/his** etc.

> Dear Laura
>   Thank you for (1) *your* letter. It was good to hear from (2) *you* and to know
> (3) .... news.
>   Let (4) .... tell you my news. In June, (5) .... sister, Sue, is getting
> married to John. Do you remember? I met John ten years ago, so he's an old friend of
> (6) .... (7)..................... are getting married in the afternoon and my parents are
> having a big party for (8) .... in the evening. (9) .... am really happy for
> her, and for John. After the wedding they are coming to stay with (10) ....
> because they haven't got a house yet. So we will all be one big, happy family.
>   My brother, Kevin, is taking (11) .... final examinations next month. After
> that (12) .... wants to get a job in a hospital. I think it will be difficult for
> (13) .... but he really wants to be a doctor. Good luck to (14) ....!
>   Last week I met Jane and Christina Sarton. Do you remember (15) ....?
> (16) .... brother was at school with us. I gave Jane your telephone number and she
> gave me (17) .... Perhaps we can all meet sometime soon.
>   I must stop now. By the way, I found a silver pen in my room. It's not
> (18) .... Is it (19) ....? I know you've got a silver one.
>   My parents send (20) .... love to you and (21) .... parents.
>   Love
>   Wendy

118 Complete the sentences. Use **himself/themselves** etc. or **by myself / by herself** etc. or **each other**.

1 He was very surprised when he looked at ..himself... in the mirror.
2 I don't like going to the cinema with other people. I prefer going ..by myself...
3 Joseph loves Christina and Christina loves Joseph. They love ..each other...
4 The child had no brothers or sisters, so she often had to play ....
5 My husband and I lived in the same street when we were children, so we saw .... very often.
6 A: Are you talking to me?
    B: No, I'm talking to ....!
7 Paul and Mike have known .... for 10 years.

Continue in the same way. Use the verbs in the box.

wrote	cut	~~lived~~	understand	enjoyed	went

8 Charles ..lived by himself... in a large house by the sea.
9 I'm afraid that the children are going to .... on the broken glass.
10 Marie speaks only French and Jill speaks only English so they can't ....
11 She didn't go to Madrid with anyone. She ....
12 We had a great time in London together. We really ....
13 Marianne and Catherine were pen friends for a long time. They .... to .... every week for 5 years.

119 What's wrong? Re-write the sentences correctly. One sentence is correct.

1 Is this book your?   _Is this book yours?_
2 Meg and I have known us for five years.   _Meg and I have known each other for five years._
3 James gave me those books. I really like it.   ....
4 Some friends of them told them the news.   ....
5 Patty gave her brother a cassette and he gave she a video.   ....
6 My brother and his wife are not happy together. They don't love themselves any more. ....
7 John is a good friend of me.   ....
8 It's your decision, not ours.   ....
9 I like this house but her windows are broken.   ....
10 I know Mary but I don't know his brother.   ....
11 I sometimes ask me why I work in a noisy, dirty city.   ....

-'s (Ann's camera) etc.

120 Complete the sentences. Use **-'s** or **-s'** + a noun.

1 David and Sue are husband and wife. David is ...Sue's husband....
2 This car belongs to Ann. It's ....
3 The king lives in a very beautiful palace. The .... is very beautiful.
4 I was with Elena at her house last night. I was at .... last night.
5 All the students have put their books on the table. All .... are on the table.
6 My sister was born on 28th June. The 28th June is ....
7 Mrs Penn makes delicious cakes. .... are delicious.
8 My grandparents have a house next door to us. My .... is next door to ours.
9 Mr and Mrs Smith have a daughter, Chris. Mr and Mrs Smith are ....

121 This is Mike and Alan's room. Whose are the objects in the room – Mike's or Alan's?

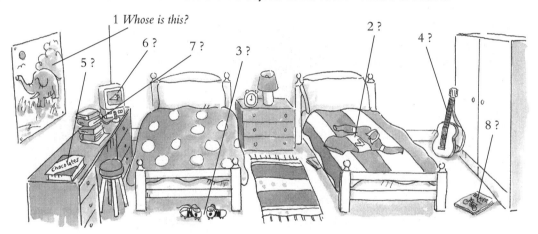

Mike likes: football, motorbikes, chocolate, wild animals.
Alan likes: reading, playing the guitar, computer games, running.

1 ..The elephant poster is Mike's...   5 ....
2 ....   6 ....
3 ....   7 ....
4 ....   8 ....

122 Complete the sentences. Use **-'s / -s' / the … of …**.

1 What's ..the name of this street?.. (the name / this street)
2 When's ..Alice's birthday?.. (the birthday / Alice)
3 Which is ....? (the favourite team / John)
4 When's ....? (the end / the programme)
5 When's ....? (the anniversary party / your parents)
6 How big are ....? (the windows / the house)
7 What's ....? (the telephone number / the station)
8 Do you know ....? (the daughter / Mr Turner)
9 Did you go to ....? (the wedding / your aunt)

a/some; countable/uncountable

Units 64–67

123 Write the opposites. Use **a** or **an**.

1 a big house
　a small house

2 a full glass

3 an easy question

4 a new book

5 a cold day

6 an expensive hotel

7 an old man

8 a light bag

124 Correct the spelling of these plurals.　　　Write the correct plural.

1 ~~watchs~~　　watches

2 knifes

3 tomatos

4 monkies

5 babys

6 ~~foots~~　　feet

7 childs

8 tooths

9 womans

10 sheeps

125 Complete the sentences. Put in **a/an/some** if necessary + words from the box.

beautiful weather	bad news	fruit	~~long hair~~	information
work	perfume	paper	new socks	new job	envelope

1 Mary's got long hair which comes half-way down her back.
2 There's .... about English courses in this book. It's quite useful.
3 I've got a card for Ian's birthday but I haven't got .... to put it in.
4 My daughter bought me .... for my birthday. It smells lovely.
5 I don't usually buy ...., but I did this morning. There was an interesting story in it.
6 A: Why is Jane crying? B: She's just had ....
7 Oh dear! Look at this hole! I need ....
8 It's .... today, isn't it? Let's go swimming.
9 I'm sure you've all got .... to do, so please be quiet and do it!
10 Julia is really happy. She's got .... in a multi-national company. It's a big change from her old one.
11 Please eat .... I bought a lot in the market today.

126 The Campbell family are packing their suitcases for their summer holiday. Here are some things they are taking with them.

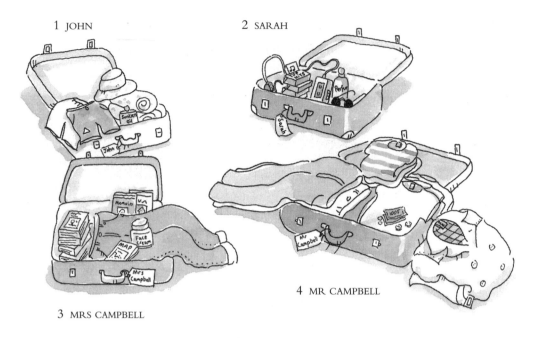

1 JOHN

2 SARAH

4 MR CAMPBELL

3 MRS CAMPBELL

Complete the sentences. Use **a(n)** / **some** / **a (two) pair(s) of ...** for each person.

1 John is taking
two pairs of shorts
a hat
some towels
some suntan oil

2 Sarah is taking
....
....
....
....

3 Mrs Campbell is taking
....
....
....
....

4 Mr Campbell is taking
....
....
....
....

☺ And you? Next month, you are going on holiday for three weeks to Australia (or the mountains of Switzerland, or Florida). Write six things that you are going to take with you.

I'm going to take
1 ....
2 ....
3 ....
4 ....
5 ....
6 ....

a/an and the

127 Put in **a/an** or **the**.

1 William wrote ..a.... letter to his bank yesterday but he forgot to post it.
   This morning, he saw ..**the**... letter on the kitchen table.
2 .... first bus in the morning leaves at 5.30 a.m.
3 When Eva White was younger she wanted to be .... musician. Now many people think
   she is .... best trumpet-player in the world.
4 I've got .... idea. Let's go to .... new Greek restaurant in Main Street tonight.
5 Julia arrived at .... station at 7 o'clock and took .... taxi to .... city centre.
6 We usually eat our meals in .... kitchen. But if we have .... guest, we eat in
   .... dining room.
7 Bern is .... capital of Switzerland. It's .... small city with about 133,000
   inhabitants.
8 My office is on .... third floor of .... old building.
9 Martin lives in .... large town in .... middle of Germany but he wants to live in
   .... country. He has got .... dog and he would like to take .... dog for long
   walks.
10 Pat watched .... science fiction movie on TV last night. .... beginning of ....
   film was fantastic but .... end was terrible.
11 I've known my husband, Sam, since I was six. We lived in .... same street when we
   were children. Sam had .... older brother, Frank. I thought he was .... most
   handsome boy in the world!
12 A: Excuse me, where's .... nearest bookshop?
   B: It's at .... end of this street, on .... left. There's .... bus-stop in front of it.

128 Read the following story. There is a word missing in some lines. Put in **a(n)** or **the** where necessary.
Some of the lines are right.

Last night, moon was shining brightly. Clare's train	(1) _the moon_
arrived at the station and she got off. She went up	(2) _right_
to station manager and asked 'Do you know if there	(3) ....
is Italian restaurant near here?' 'Yes, it's very	(4) ....
near, just about 200 metres on left, opposite	(5) ....
Information Centre.' 'Thank you,' said Clare and	(6) ....
she started walking. She found restaurant and went	(7) ....
inside. There was woman playing the piano, and	(8) ....
there, in the corner of the room next to kitchen, was	(9) ....
Ron Allen – just man she wanted to see. He was	(10) ....
eating dinner, but when he saw Clare he stopped.	(11) ....
He thought she looked exactly same – beautiful and	(12) ....
calm. 'Have you got papers?' he asked. 'No, I haven't.	(13) ....
I've given them to police,' she replied. 'I hope they	(14) ....
will arrest you and send you to prison.' When he heard	(15) ....
her words, Ron jumped up, took knife from the table	(16) ....
and ran out. But outside …	

129 Complete the sentences with the words in brackets ( ). Use **the** where necessary.

1 Martin enjoys listening to ..*music*.. but he doesn't really like ..*the music*.. that his son plays on his guitar. (music)

2 .... is one of my favourite sports. (football)

3 Joe wasn't interested in .... when he was at school but he's just read a book about .... of the South American Indians and he really enjoyed it. (history)

4 I must show you .... of our holiday in Ireland. Pat's really very good at taking .... (photos)

5 .... opposite my house blew down in the wind last night. I don't think it's a good idea to have .... near houses. (trees)

6 Sarah loves .... When she visits foreign countries, she always goes to local restaurants and tries .... which is typical of that region. (food)

7 A: What's good on the menu today?
   B: .... is excellent.
   A: I'm afraid I don't eat .... (chicken)

8 David spends a lot of time travelling on business. He enjoys staying in .... (hotels)

9 A: Did Chloe return .... she borrowed from you last week?
   B: Yes. I told her, 'I need it back. .... doesn't grow on trees!' (money)

130

A Here is some information about a famous river. Put in **the** where necessary.

(1) ..*The*.. Amazon is in (2) .... South America. It begins near (3) .... west of the continent, 160 kms from (4) .... Pacific Ocean. It starts in (5) .... Andes in (6) .... Peru and then it flows through (7) .... Brazil and out into (8) .... Atlantic.

B Now read about London. Put in **the** where necessary before the names of the famous places.

Most people want to see where the Queen lives when they visit (9) ..—.. London, so (10) .... Buckingham Palace is very popular. But I think the best thing to do is to take a boat trip on (11) .... River Thames to see all the famous buildings. You can get on the boat at (12) .... Westminster Bridge, near (13) .... Houses of Parliament. If you go down the river to (14) .... Tower of London, you will pass (15) .... St Paul's Cathedral on the way. This is a very old and beautiful church, and my favourite building.
As a change from sightseeing, you could go shopping along (16) .... Oxford Street, or maybe if you like animals, go to (17) .... London Zoo.
There's a lot to do and see in the capital. Come and see!

☺ And in your country?

What's the capital city? ....
Name one important street in your capital. ....
What's the most famous building? ....
What's your favourite building? ....
What's the name of the building that your government works in? ....

some and any

131 Put in **some** or **any**.

DAN: Let's go for a picnic by the river tomorrow.
RUTH: OK. We'll make (1) _some_ sandwiches. What do we need?
DAN: We haven't got (2) .... bread. Can you buy (3) ....?
RUTH: Yes, sure. What about butter?
DAN: We've got (4) .... I'll buy (5) .... cheese.
RUTH: OK, and is there (6) .... orange juice in the fridge?
DAN: No, I'll get (7) ....
RUTH: Good. Do we need (8) .... apples or cherries?
DAN: Just (9) .... apples.
RUTH: Oh dear! I haven't got (10) .... money to buy the bread!
DAN: Don't worry. I'll lend you (11) ....

132 Complete these sentences. Use **some** or **any** + a suitable noun.

1 Leo has gone to the bank to get _some money._
2 Can I have .... in my tea? I don't like it black.
3 I'd like .... about hotels in London, please.
4 I want to light the barbecue but I haven't got ....
5 Clare is not very happy with her maths exam. She knows she made ....
6 Can I borrow ....? I need to wash my hair.
7 Sorry, but everyone has to sit on the floor. We haven't got .... yet.
8 There wasn't .... in my village last winter so we couldn't go skiing.
9 Can I have .... on my bread? I prefer strawberry if you have it.

133 Put in **somebody** (or **someone**) / **something** / **anybody** (or **anyone**) / **anything**.

1 I feel a bit sick. I think I've eaten _something_ bad.
2 Did .... telephone me last night?
3 A: What's the matter? B: I think there's .... in the garden.
4 A: What's wrong? B: I've put .... in my coffee, and it wasn't sugar!
5 Please don't tell .... about the letter. It's a secret.
6 You look bored. Would you like .... to do?
7 Has .... seen my bicycle? It's not in the garage.
8 There isn't .... to watch on TV tonight. Let's go out.
9 .... dropped a £10 note in the street outside my house yesterday.
10 I don't think I've learnt .... from his lecture.

some/any/no/none

134 Re-write these sentences. Use **any** or **no**.

1 There isn't any milk in the fridge. *There's no milk in the fridge.*
2 We had no electricity last night. *We didn't have any electricity last night.*
3 I haven't got any grandparents. ....
4 There's no time to visit the museums. ....
5 We didn't have any rain in July last year. ....
6 There are no clouds in the sky today. ....
7 There was no sugar in my tea. ....
8 Tim hasn't got any books in his house. ....

135 Right or wrong? Correct the underlined word where necessary. Use **some/any/no/none**. Three sentences are right.

1 Mary hasn't got <u>some</u> stamps in her purse. *..any..*
2 There aren't <u>no</u> easy questions. ....
3 A: How many books did you read on holiday? B: <u>None</u>. ....
4 Would you like <u>some</u> ice-cream? ....
5 Please don't offer me any chocolates. I don't want <u>none</u>. ....
6 I didn't give him <u>no</u> money. ....
7 Have you written <u>any</u> postcards yet? ....
8 There are <u>any</u> biscuits in the tin. We must buy some. ....
9 Can I have <u>any</u> potatoes, please? ....

136 Complete the conversation between Jenny and her friend, Martin. Use **some/any/no/none**.

JENNY: Hi, Martin. How are you?
MARTIN: Fine, but busy. We've got (1) ..some.. exams next week – remember?
JENNY: I know. How much work did you do last night?
MARTIN: (2) ...., I went to the cinema. What about you?
JENNY: I had (3) .... time last night. It was my sister's birthday so we all went out for dinner.
MARTIN: Have you done (4) .... work this morning?
JENNY: (5) ...., but not a lot. Anyway, I rang to ask you something. Do you know where my physics book is?
MARTIN: I've got (6) .... idea, but you can borrow mine if you want.
JENNY: Thanks.
MARTIN: Let's meet outside Natbank in the High Street this lunchtime. I need to get (7) .... money and I'll bring my physics book for you.
JENNY: Good idea. I'm very worried about the physics exam. Have you got (8) .... old exam papers? I'd really like to look at them.
MARTIN: I haven't got (9) .... but my brother's got (10) .... from 1995. I'll bring them with me at lunchtime.
JENNY: Wonderful! See you at 12.30. OK?

somebody/anything/nowhere etc.

137 Put in **anybody (anyone)** / **anything** / **nobody (no-one)** / **nothing**.

1 There was a thunderstorm during the night but I heard .....*nothing.*.....
2 There isn't .... I like on the menu.
3 Fred isn't a nice person. .... likes him.
4 I can't hear .... Can you turn the radio up?
5 Sheila's lonely in London because she doesn't know ....
6 What's that in your hand? ....
7 I haven't bought .... for Sarah's birthday.
8 .... can help you. You must do it yourself.
9 A: What are you doing tonight? B: ....
10 Ken was in hospital for two days but .... went to see him.
11 There wasn't .... in the cinema. It was completely empty.

138 Put in **somebody/anything/nowhere** etc.

> *Dear Phil*
> *I've been here for two months and I don't like this place. I haven't met* (1) ....*anybody*......
> *interesting. Also, it's very quiet in the evenings. All the shops and restaurants close early and*
> *the streets are empty. There's* (2) .... *to go and there is* (3) ....
> *good on TV.*
>   *Then yesterday* (4) .... *told me about a sports club* (5) ....
> *near my house. So I decided to try it. I found it – it's only ten minutes from my house and it's*
> *great. There's weight-training, tennis, a swimming pool, and the people there are very*
> *friendly.* (6) .... *tells you what to do – you can choose for yourself. In the*
> *middle of the evening,* (7) .... *said, 'Hello, I'm Tony. Are you doing*
> (8) .... *later this evening? Would you like to go for* (9) ....
> *to eat?' I said, 'Yes, I'd love to.'*
>   *We had delicious pizzas and that night I thought to myself, 'This town is getting better! I*
> *haven't been* (10) .... *for two months and now I've been to two new places*
> *in one evening and made a friend.'*
>   *All the best*
>   *Geoffrey*

139   Complete the sentences. Use **somebody/anything/nowhere** etc. + **to ...** (e.g. **to go / to stay / to eat**).

SUE: I'm hungry.
DAD: Would you like (1) _something to eat?_
SUE: Yes, please.

FRED: I'm bored. I've got (2) ....
MUM: Go and play tennis.
FRED: All my friends are on holiday so I haven't got (3) .... with.

KEN: Let's have lunch in this restaurant.
MEG: It looks very busy. Is there (4) ....?
KEN: Yes, there are two seats over there.

LIZ: We're going to Rome in September.
TIM: Wonderful.
LIZ: Yes, but we've got a problem. We haven't got (5) .... yet.
TIM: Have you tried The Plaza Hotel? They usually have free rooms.

PAM: I'm going to a really important party at the weekend and I need
       (6) ....
CAROL: You can borrow my new black dress if you want.

TANYA: Jerry, go and talk to Annie. She's in the kitchen.
JERRY: I haven't got (7) ....
TANYA: Of course you have! You always have lots to say. Go and talk about food or sport.

every and **all**   Unit 79

140   Complete the sentences with **every** + the correct form of the verb.

1   There are no losers in our competition. _Every_ child _wins_ (win) a prize.
2   When I was at school, ... teacher .... (be) female.
3   .... mountain in the Himalayas .... (be) over 3,000 metres.
4   .... car in our showroom .... (have) got a sun-roof, radio-cassette and electric windows.
5   I loved going to my grandparents' house when they were alive. .... room .... (be) filled with beautiful furniture.

141   Complete the sentences with **every/all** + the word in brackets ( ).

(morning)
1   It was raining yesterday, so I wrote letters _all morning._
2   .... I catch the number 91 bus to the supermarket.
3   Jane waited .... for the electrician to arrive. He came at 2.30 p.m.

(summer)
4   When I was a child, my family and I went to the same place for holidays ....
5   This year the weather has been terrible. I don't think we've seen the sun ....
6   David has got exams in the autumn so he'll have to study ....

(night)

7 .... last week Kate had the same dream.

8 My neighbours had a party on Saturday. The noise was terrible and I was awake

....

9 A: Why are you so tired this morning? B: I didn't go to bed. I worked ....

(day)

10 I want to keep fit so I try to go jogging ....

11 I'm really hungry. I haven't eaten ....

12 Jack doesn't go to the office .... Some days he works at home.

---

142 Put in **everybody** (or **everyone**) / **everywhere** / **everything** + a verb.

1 A: These shirts are expensive.
B: _Everything is_ expensive in this shop.

2 A: Why are so many people wearing black?
B: Because it's fashionable. .... wearing black this year.

3 A: Do you always watch ice-hockey on TV?
B: Yes, ... in my family .... it. We love it.

4 A: Did you enjoy your day in London?
B: Yes, very much, but .... really busy because it was school holiday time.

5 A: My grandfather says that family life was better when he was young.
B: Yes, a lot of old people think that .... better in the past.

6 A: Things in our country seem to be changing quickly at the moment.
B: Well, it's not only our country. .... changing.

---

all/most/some/any/no/none

143 Complete the sentences. Use the word in brackets ( ). Sometimes you need of (**some of** / **none of** etc.).

1 My children were quiet _all_ the time I was at the dentist.   (all)

2 .... the passengers got off the bus in the city centre.   (most)

3 .... these books are not yours. You must take them back to the library.   (some)

4 I haven't read .... books by Agatha Christie.   (any)

5 .... these papers must leave this room. They're secret.   (none)

6 I think .... children like ice-cream, don't they?   (all)

7 You can buy .... the things you want in our local supermarket.   (most)

8 .... sportsmen and women receive a lot of money.   (some)

9 .... Jack's friends came to see him when he was ill.   (none)

10 When my father was young, there were .... cinemas in the town.   (no)

11 Linda has got some strange friends. I don't really like .... them.   (any)

12 My grandfather lived in the same house .... his life.   (all)

144 Write sentences. Use **all/most/some/none**.

> Richard is 40 years old. He's a manager in a large multi-national company. He and the people who work in his company answered some questions about their health.
>
> | | **Yes** |
> |------------------------------|---------|
> | Do you take regular exercise? | 63% |
> | Do you walk to work? | 25% |
> | Have you got a car? | 100% |
> | Do you use your car every day? | 80% |

1 *Most of Richard's colleagues take regular exercise.*

2 ....

3 ....

4 ....

> Lisa is 16 years old and she's a high school student. Read the answers that she and her friends gave to some different questions.
>
> | | **Yes** |
> |--------------------------------|---------|
> | Do you go to the cinema every month? | 37% |
> | Do you play some kind of sport? | 100% |
> | Do you study every night? | 0% |
> | Do you enjoy dancing? | 67% |

5 ....

6 ....

7 ....

8 ....

145 Write answers to these questions. Choose from **all/most/some/none** + **of it / of them**.

1 How many exercises in this book have you done?   *Some of them.*

2 How much of your work/study do you enjoy? ....

3 How many of the people in your street do you know? ....

4 How many houses in your street have got gardens? ....

5 How many families living near you have got young children? ....

6 How much of today's newspaper have you read? ....

7 How much of this exercise do you think you've done correctly? ....

both/either/neither

146 Put in **both/either/neither**. Use **of** where necessary.

1 A: Do you like pop music or jazz.
    B: I don't like *either of* them. I prefer classical music.

2 A: Jill looks tired.
    B: Yes, *both* her children are in bed ill.

3 A: Where would you like to go for your holidays this year? Greece or Spain?
    B: .... is fine with me. I like them both.

4 A: Which question did you answer, number 1 or number 3?
    B: .... I answered number 4.

5 A: Why's Jane in hospital?
    B: She had an accident yesterday and broke .... her legs.

(night)

7 .... last week Kate had the same dream.

8 My neighbours had a party on Saturday. The noise was terrible and I was awake
....

9 A: Why are you so tired this morning? B: I didn't go to bed. I worked ....

(day)

10 I want to keep fit so I try to go jogging ....

11 I'm really hungry. I haven't eaten ....

12 Jack doesn't go to the office .... Some days he works at home.

---

142 Put in **everybody** (or **everyone**) / **everywhere** / **everything** + a verb.

1 A: These shirts are expensive.
 B: *Everything is* expensive in this shop.

2 A: Why are so many people wearing black?
 B: Because it's fashionable. .... wearing black this year.

3 A: Do you always watch ice-hockey on TV?
 B: Yes, ... in my family .... it. We love it.

4 A: Did you enjoy your day in London?
 B: Yes, very much, but .... really busy because it was school holiday time.

5 A: My grandfather says that family life was better when he was young.
 B: Yes, a lot of old people think that .... better in the past.

6 A: Things in our country seem to be changing quickly at the moment.
 B: Well, it's not only our country. .... changing.

---

all/most/some/any/no/none   Unit 80

143 Complete the sentences. Use the word in brackets ( ). Sometimes you need **of** (**some of** / **none of** etc.).

1 My children were quiet *all* the time I was at the dentist.   (all)

2 .... the passengers got off the bus in the city centre.   (most)

3 .... these books are not yours. You must take them back to the library.   (some)

4 I haven't read .... books by Agatha Christie.   (any)

5 .... these papers must leave this room. They're secret.   (none)

6 I think .... children like ice-cream, don't they?   (all)

7 You can buy .... the things you want in our local supermarket.   (most)

8 .... sportsmen and women receive a lot of money.   (some)

9 .... Jack's friends came to see him when he was ill.   (none)

10 When my father was young, there were .... cinemas in the town.   (no)

11 Linda has got some strange friends. I don't really like .... them.   (any)

12 My grandfather lived in the same house .... his life.   (all)

144 Write sentences. Use **all/most/some/none**.

Richard is 40 years old. He's a manager in a large multi-national company. He and the people who work in his company answered some questions about their health.

	Yes
Do you take regular exercise?	63%
Do you walk to work?	25%
Have you got a car?	100%
Do you use your car every day?	80%

1 *Most of Richard's colleagues take regular exercise.*
2 ....
3 ....
4 ....

Lisa is 16 years old and she's a high school student. Read the answers that she and her friends gave to some different questions.

	Yes
Do you go to the cinema every month?	37%
Do you play some kind of sport?	100%
Do you study every night?	0%
Do you enjoy dancing?	67%

5 ....
6 ....
7 ....
8 ....

145 Write answers to these questions. Choose from **all/most/some/none** + **of it / of them**.

1 How many exercises in this book have you done?   *Some of them.*
2 How much of your work/study do you enjoy?   ....
3 How many of the people in your street do you know?   ....
4 How many houses in your street have got gardens?   ....
5 How many families living near you have got young children?   ....
6 How much of today's newspaper have you read?   ....
7 How much of this exercise do you think you've done correctly?   ....

both/either/neither

146 Put in **both/either/neither**. Use **of** where necessary.

1 A: Do you like pop music or jazz.
   B: I don't like ...*either of*... them. I prefer classical music.

2 A: Jill looks tired.
   B: Yes, ...*both*... her children are in bed ill.

3 A: Where would you like to go for your holidays this year? Greece or Spain?
   B: .... is fine with me. I like them both.

4 A: Which question did you answer, number 1 or number 3?
   B: .... I answered number 4.

5 A: Why's Jane in hospital?
   B: She had an accident yesterday and broke .... her legs.

6 A: Would you like potatoes or rice with your chicken?
   B: ...., please! I'm really hungry.

7 A: I enjoyed both those films.
   B: Did you? I didn't like .... them.

8 A: Did you know Jimmy or John when you were younger?
   B: They lived in the same street as me so I knew .... them.

9 A: Hurry up! We're going to be late. What's the problem?
   B: .... these shirts is the right colour. I need a blue one.

10 A: Have you read the latest two postcards from Mary in the States?
    B: No, I haven't read .... them, yet.

---

147 Write sentences about yourself and one of your friends. Think of some things which are similar in your lives. Use **Both of us / Neither of us ....**

1 Both of us live in apartments.
2 Neither of us has (got) a dog.

☺ 3 ....   6 ....
   4 ....   7 ....
   5 ....   8 ....

---

a lot / much / many; (a) little / (a) few

148 Look at the picture and see what is left after the wedding party is finished. Write sentences.
Use: **There aren't many ... / There isn't much ... / There isn't/aren't any ....**

1 There isn't much champagne.   5 ....
2 ....   6 ....
3 ....   7 ....
4 ....

149 Liz is asking you some questions. Write questions with **How much/many ...?** Then write your own answers. Use **a lot / not (very) much / not (very) many / a few / a little / none**.

1 LIZ: (books / be / on your table?)   *How many books are there on your table?*
   YOU: *Not many.*

2 LIZ: (milk / you / like / in your coffee?) .... ?
   YOU: ....

3 LIZ: (cars / you / see / out of the window?) .... ?
   YOU: ....

4 LIZ: (money / you / spend / in one month?) .... ?
   YOU: ....

5 LIZ: (good friends / you / have?) .... ?
   YOU: ....

6 LIZ: (football / you / play?) .... ?
   YOU: ....

7 LIZ: (pairs of socks / you / have?) .... ?
   YOU: ....

8 LIZ: (fruit / you / eat / every day?) .... ?
   YOU: ....

9 LIZ: (water / you / drink / every day?) .... ?
   YOU: ....

150 Complete the text about Antarctica. Put in **little / a little**, **few / a few**.

Antarctica is a snow-covered continent. The average temperature at the South Pole is –51°C. (1) *Few* plants or animals can live on the land – it is too cold for them. The animal life is found on and in the sea. There are (2) .... scientists from different countries who live and work on special bases in Antarctica. On midsummer's day (December 22nd) there is daylight for 24 hours and so during this period (3) .... tourist ships and planes come to see this strange land. But in the winter there is (4) .... daylight for months. It must be a terrible place during the winter. The snow is always there – winter and summer – but in fact (5) .... snow falls in the year (an average of 12 – 20 cm). People say that it can be a beautiful place. At first, it appears frightening but after (6) .... time, some people fall in love with it.

old, nice etc. (adjectives); quickly, badly etc. (adverbs)

151 Complete the story about Jane's visit to China. Use the adjectives from the box + a suitable noun.

delicious	~~long~~	famous	old	big	difficult	friendly	hot	busy

Yesterday, Jane Greenwood flew back to London from China. It was a very (1) .lo̲ng̲ fli̲g̲h̲t̲ – 20 hours – and she feels tired today.

She was on holiday in China. She stayed in an (2) .... Three hundred years ago an emperor built it. The only problem was that there was no (3) .... in the rooms so everybody had cold showers. She visited many (4) ...., for example, The Great Wall of China. She ate some (5) .... Her favourite was egg fried rice. She met a lot of very (6) .... Jane can't speak Chinese so they spoke to her in English. She tried a few words in Chinese but people said it is a (7) .... to learn.

A lot of things in China surprised her. For example, the (8) .... There were hundreds and hundreds of bicycles on the roads all day and all night. There was never a quiet moment.

Jane wants to go back to China next year. She knows it is a (9) .... and she only saw a small part of it.

152 Complete the sentences with an adjective, an adverb or a noun.

1 John is sometimes a dangerous .d̲r̲i̲v̲e̲r̲.... I think he drives .d̲a̲n̲g̲e̲r̲o̲u̲s̲l̲y̲... when he's in a hurry.
2 Pam's old car was slow but her new one is very .f̲a̲s̲t̲....
3 James looked .... when his team won the game.
4 It rained .... all day yesterday and the ground was very wet.
5 Mmmmm, what a wonderful .... from the kitchen. What are you cooking? I'm sure it's going to taste ....
6 I think Mrs Burns is a good .... She taught my children ....
7 David hasn't got a lot of money so when he goes shopping he always looks .... at the prices.
8 My parents were hard .... They worked .... all their lives.
9 Jackie did .... in his test and had to take it again.
10 I spoke to Peter on the telephone this morning. He sounded really .... Someone stole his car yesterday.

153 Complete the conversation with **well** or **good**.

LAURA: You don't look very (1) _well_. Are you ill?
DIANA: No, I'm just a bit tired.
LAURA: Did you enjoy the party last night?
DIANA: Yes, it was very (2) .... Did you?
LAURA: Yes, very much. John plays the piano really (3) ...., doesn't he?
DIANA: Mmmm. I didn't know he was (4) .... at the piano.
LAURA: His sister's a (5) .... player too.
DIANA: Was she there last night?
LAURA: No, she wasn't feeling (6) ...., so she didn't come. I think she's got a bad cold.
DIANA: I don't remember her very (7) .... Was she at school with us?
LAURA: Yes, but she wasn't in the same class.
DIANA: You've got a (8) .... memory!

older/oldest (comparatives and superlatives)

154 Write sentences with **not as … as** and the comparative (**older / more difficult** etc.).

1 (Mexico City / London / expensive / crowded)
    Mexico City isn't as expensive as London but it is more crowded.

2 (city life / village life / friendly / exciting)

3 (motorways / country roads / interesting / fast)

4 (travelling by plane / travelling by bus / cheap / comfortable)

5 (Egypt / Iceland / green / warm)

6 (bicycles / cars / comfortable / easy to park)

155 Only two of these comparative sentences are correct. Correct the mistakes where necessary.

1 He got up more early than she did.   _He got up earlier than she did._
2 My computer is moderner than yours.   ....
3 Jack is a more good player than me.   ....
4 It's a bit hotter today.   ....
5 Is it more interesting as his last book?   ....
6 He paid less than you for the ticket.   ....
7 My mother is the same age like my father.   ....
8 Ann's headache is badder today.   ....
9 She lives much more far away now.   ....

156   Read the following comparison between the USA and Australia. Fill in the gaps with one word only.

The USA has a much (1) *bigger* population (2) .... Australia, and American cities are (3) .... crowded than Australian ones.

There are not (4) .... many mountains in Australia (5) .... in the USA. Both countries have deserts and beautiful beaches. But America has many (6) .... rivers than Australia.

The northern and central parts of the USA have much (7) .... snow in winter than anywhere in Australia and generally these two areas have a (8) .... winter than Australia does. Australia is in the southern hemisphere and doesn't have its winter at the same time (9) .... countries in the northern hemisphere.

Most people in these countries speak the same language (10) .... each other – English – but their accents are very different. Some people say that the Americans are warmer and (11) .... friendly (12) .... the Australians but I don't see any difference.

☺ Now you write some sentences comparing your country with another country that you know. Use the paragraph about the USA and Australia to help you. Write about:

 – the geography (rivers, mountains, cities, etc.)
 – the weather (hot, wet, dry, cold, etc.)
 – the people (language, character, etc.)

....
....
....

157   Comparing now and then. Albert is thinking about life today and life 40 years ago. Complete his sentences. Use **... than** or **not as ... as**.

1 (cars / fast)   *Cars are faster than they were.*
2 (children / more things)   *Children have got more things than they had.*
3 (people / not work / hard)   *People don't work as hard as they did.*
4 (life / expensive)   ....
5 (people / not / friendly)   ....
6 (films / violent)   ....
7 (people / live / long)   ....
8 (house / good)   ....
9 (families / not big)   ....
10 (children / freedom)   ....
11 (people / eat / good food)   ....

158　Terry is asking you some questions about your life.
Write his questions. Use the superlative + the present perfect
(e.g. **the most beautiful … you've ever seen**).
Answer the questions in your own words.

1　TERRY:　(What / good / holiday / you have?)
　　　　　What's the best holiday you've had?
　YOU:　*My holiday in Greece last year.*

2　TERRY:　(Who / interesting person / you / meet?)
　　　　　...?
　YOU:　...

3　TERRY:　(What / frightening experience / you / have?)
　　　　　...?
　YOU:　...

4　TERRY:　(What / bad film / you / see?)
　　　　　...?
　YOU:　...

5　TERRY:　(What / expensive thing / you / buy?)
　　　　　...?
　YOU:　...

6　TERRY:　(What / unusual food / you / eat?)
　　　　　...?
　YOU:　...

7　TERRY:　(Which / large city / you / go to?)
　　　　　...?
　YOU:　...

8　TERRY:　(What / useful present / you / receive?)
　　　　　...?
　YOU:　...

enough and too　　　　　　　　　　　　　　　　　　　**Units 90–91**

159　Complete the sentences. Use **enough** + one of the words from the box.

people	~~good~~	fit	~~money~~	plates	sweet	information	study

1　Have you got ...*enough money*... to pay for all these things?
2　My English is not ...*good enough*... for an interpreter's job.
3　We had 12 people for dinner last night but we didn't have ....!
4　Jane didn't pass her examination because she didn't ....
5　The party on Saturday was very quiet. There weren't .... there.
6　Is your tea ...., or would you like some more sugar?
7　I can't give you an answer because I haven't got ....
8　William couldn't run more than 200 metres because he wasn't ....

Now use **enough** + one of the words from the box + **to** (**do**, **eat**, **drive**, etc.).

money	~~old~~	well	time	sharp	warm

9 Mary is 14 years old. She isn't _old enough to drive_ a car.
10 I can't use this knife. It's not .... the meat.
11 Oh dear! I haven't got .... Pete a birthday present. Can you lend me some?
12 You should stay in bed. You don't look .... to Tina's party.
13 That was a horrible test. Did you have .... all the questions?
14 It's only 13 degrees. It's not .... in the garden.

160 Complete the sentences. Use **too** / **too much** / **too many**.

1 Aunt Mary didn't buy the dress because it _was too_ expensive.
2 Carl felt ill last night because he _had (or ate) too many_ chocolates.
3 Jim doesn't use his bicycle in town because .... dangerous.
4 I didn't enjoy shopping in the market because there .... people.
5 We don't usually go to the beach at midday because it .... hot.
6 And he didn't sleep very well because he .... coffee.
7 I can't see anything because .... dark.
8 Ann doesn't like swimming in the sea because .... cold.

161 Peter lives in an old city which is very popular with tourists. He doesn't like it. Here are some of his reasons:

1 a lot of cars
2 very narrow streets
3 only 3 cinemas
4 a lot of noise and dirt
5 the parks are very small
6 very few things to do after work
7 a lot of tourists

Complete Peter's sentences. Use **too** or **enough**.

1 _There are too many cars._
2 _The streets are not wide enough._ or _The streets are too narrow._
3 There ....
4 There ....
5 The ....
6 There ....
7 There ....

☺ What about the place where you live? Are there some things you don't like? Use **too** and **enough** to write about your city / town / village.

....
....

162 When are you allowed to do certain things?

In Britain, at the age of:
5 – You start primary school.
12 – You can buy a pet (e.g. a dog or a cat).
13 – You can work for two hours a day.
16 – You can leave school.
   – You can get married with your parents' permission.
17 – You can drive a car.
18 – You can vote.
21 – You can become a Member of Parliament.

Use the information to say whether these people are old enough to do what they want.
Use **too** or **enough**.

1 John is only 3 years old and he wants to go to school. Can he?
    No, he's too young to go to school. or *He's not old enough to go to school.*
2 My daughter is 14. Can she work in a shop after school?
    Yes, she's old enough to work for two hours a day.
3 Can Jane and Terry get married? They are 15.
    .... or ....
4 Can Peter start driving lessons? He's 17.
    ....
5 Barbara's 10 and she wants to buy a dog with her own money. Can she buy one?
    .... or ....
6 Eric is 16 and is fed up with school. Can he leave?
    ....
7 Ann is only 20 but she is very interested in politics and what is happening in her country. Can she become a Member of Parliament?
    .... or ....

Word order; still/yet/already

163 Put the words in the right order where necessary. One sentence is right.

1 Rachel often is late for school.   *Rachel is often late for school.*
2 I already have won two tennis championships. ....
3 Maria goes rarely to bed before midnight. ....
4 My children? They are all adults now. ....
5 My brother and I live still at home. ....
6 When do you do usually your homework? ....
7 I never can remember my car registration number. ....
8 My sister sometimes is horrible to me. ....
9 Clare speaks Spanish and she understands also Italian. ....
10 John and Steve? They both are married now. ....
11 My younger brother just has finished school. ....

164 Complete the sentences. Use **still**.

1 It started snowing two hours ago and it is ..*still snowing*.. heavily.
2 John bought an old car in 1990 and he .... today.
3 I know she said she was sorry, but I .... angry.
4 My father first went to a football game in 1975 and he .... every week.
5 I know you went swimming regularly when you were younger. Do you
.... every day?
6 Monica felt ill two days ago and went to bed. She .... in bed.

165 Complete the sentences with the verb in brackets ( ). Use **still** (+ positive) and **yet** (+ negative).

1 TEACHER: OK everyone. Stop now. Please give me your test papers.
  STUDENT: Sorry, I _*haven't finished yet*_ (finish) _*I am still writing.*_ (write)
2 A: Come on, we're going to be late.
  B: I .... keys. (look for)
  I .... (find)
3 Dear Sue
  The weather continues to be wet. It .... (rain)
  We .... (see the sun)
4 A: (*on the phone*) You sound very sleepy.
  B: Yes, I .... (get up)
  I .... bed. (be)
5 A: Are you and Tony friends again?
  B: No. He .... (apologise)
  I .... angry. (be)

---

at, until, before etc. (prepositions of time)   Units 96–98

166 Complete the sentences. Choose from the boxes.

at on in	+	night six weeks winter Thursday midnight 1900 Christmas 6.30 a.m. ~~evening~~ November 22nd 1963

1 After working all day, John is too tired to go out .*in the evening*...
2 Last night I went to bed ....
3 President Kennedy was shot ....
4 In Christian countries, most people don't work ....
5 Our cat stays out .... and comes back home in the morning.
6 Jill loves skiing so she usually takes her holidays sometime ....
7 My parents' alarm clock always rings ....
8 Her grandfather was born .... so he is now a very old man.
9 Mary is expecting a baby .... so she'll finish working soon.
10 I have a lecture .... so I can't meet you then, I'm afraid.

167 Complete the sentences with words from the box. In **one** sentence, no word is necessary.

at	on	in	until	since	for	from	to

1 Pat's uncle left Canada ..in... 1968 and went to Brazil.
2 John is getting married .... the end of the month.
3 The accident happened .... Monday morning when Sue was driving to work.
4 Alan has been feeling sick .... he ate some fish last night.
5 Are you going to stay .... the end of the film?
6 The birds started singing .... half past four this morning.
7 We'll know the result of the exam .... three weeks.
8 An American player won the tennis championship .... Independence Day.
9 Robert is going to stop work .... next February.
10 I swim in the sea every day .... summer.
11 Does John really enjoy working .... night?
12 A: How long are you going to stay here? B: .... I can speak the language perfectly.
13 Kate went to Istanbul .... four days last spring.
14 Mark works hard .... Monday .... Friday, so he sleeps .... the weekend.

168 Complete the story of Jess Brewer's life. Use words from the box.

during	for	~~from~~	after	to	until	before	while	since

Jess Brewer was a pupil at her local school (1) ..from.. 1975 (2) .... 1988. (3) .... her last year at
school she taught herself how to use computers, and this knowledge was very useful for her later.
(4) .... leaving school, she went to university and studied mathematics. She was responsible for
producing a student magazine on her computer (5) .... she was there. She stayed at university
(6) .... four years and then decided to travel (7) .... finding a job.
    She has been working as a computer programmer (8) .... she came back from her travels,
but she wants to go away again. She knows that she has to stay with the computer company
(9) .... she has enough money to go and do what she wants.

169 Jess is describing a normal day in her life. Complete her story. Use words from the box.

at	on	in	since	for	until	from
during	while	after	to	before		

I wake up (1) ..at.. about 7.30 a.m. (2) ..during.. the week, but much later (3) .... Saturdays.
(4) .... I wake up, I move very fast. In fact, I'm very good (5) .... the mornings. I only need
20 minutes (6) .... the time my alarm clock rings (7) .... the time I leave the house. I don't
have breakfast at home; I have to wait (8) .... I arrive at the office for a cup of coffee.
    I start work (9) .... 9.00 a.m. and work (10) .... four hours. (11) .... lunchtime, I often
sit in the park and read (12) .... I am eating my sandwiches. (13) .... going back to the office,
I do some shopping. The afternoon passes very quickly. I work (14) .... 6 o'clock and then I go
home. I've been working for the same company (15) .... 1994.
    (16) .... the evenings, I usually watch TV or maybe go out for dinner with some friends. I
don't go to bed late because I have to get up for work the next day. (17) .... the weekends, my
routine is very different.

in, under, through etc. (prepositions of place and direction)

Units 96–98

☺ Now write a paragraph about a normal day in your life. The following ideas will help you.

wake up / get up?	work / school	afternoon?	bed?
breakfast?	lunchtime?	evenings?	

I usually wake up ...

....

....

---

in, under, through etc. (prepositions of place and direction)

Units 99–103

170 Some customers in the supermarket can't find what they want. You are the assistant. Complete the sentences.

1 I can't find the cereals.
   YOU: They're ..*on*.. the left, ..*on*.. the bottom shelf, ..*below*.. the sugar.

2 Where's the rice, please?
   YOU: It's .... the left, ... the top shelf, ... the pasta and the bread.

3 Where are the biscuits, please?
   YOU: They're .... the right, ... shelf, ... the nuts.

4 Where's the water, please?
   YOU: It's .... the right, ... shelf, ... the cola.

5 I can't find the tea.
   YOU: It's .... the right, ... shelf, ... the cola.

6 And the cakes?
   YOU: They're .... the cola, ... shelf, ... middle, ... the biscuits and the chocolate.

Now you say where the coffee is.

7 The coffee is ....

And the flour?

8 The flour is ....

87

171 Look at John's travel plans for September. Complete his story using **to/in/at** if necessary. In one sentence no preposition is necessary.

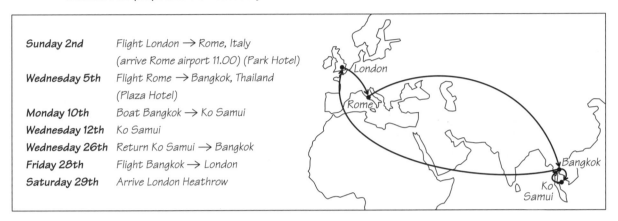

Sunday 2nd	Flight London → Rome, Italy
	(arrive Rome airport 11.00) (Park Hotel)
Wednesday 5th	Flight Rome → Bangkok, Thailand
	(Plaza Hotel)
Monday 10th	Boat Bangkok → Ko Samui
Wednesday 12th	Ko Samui
Wednesday 26th	Return Ko Samui → Bangkok
Friday 28th	Flight Bangkok → London
Saturday 29th	Arrive London Heathrow

I'm flying (1) .**to**.. Italy on Sunday 2nd September, and the plane arrives (2) .... Rome airport at 11.00. I'm staying (3) .... Rome (4) .... the Park Hotel for three days. Then, on Wednesday, I'm going (5) .... Thailand for five days. I'll arrive (6) .... the Plaza Hotel (7) .... the centre of Bangkok late on Wednesday evening. On Saturday I'm meeting a friend of mine (8) .... the hotel. He lives (9) .... the north of Thailand and is coming (10) .... Bangkok. We are going on holiday together.

On Monday the 10th, we are taking a boat (11) .... one of the islands, Ko Samui. The journey takes three days so we arrive there on Wednesday evening. We're staying there for two weeks. It's going to be wonderful. On the 26th we return by boat and get back (12) .... Bangkok on the 28th. Early the next day I fly back (13) .... England. I arrive (14) .... home in the middle of the night. A wonderful month for me!

172 A visit from the neighbour's cat. Look at the journey that Felix made in Sue's garden. Complete the story with prepositions (**over / up / out of / into** etc.).

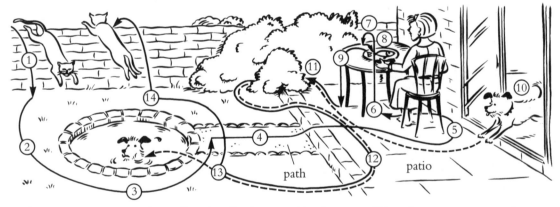

Felix jumped (1) .**over**... the wall and walked (2) .**across**... the grass. Then he went (3) .... the pond and (4) .... the path. He walked (5) .... Sue's chair and (6) .... the table. Suddenly he jumped (7) .... the table and took the fish which was (8) .... Sue's plate. He jumped (9) .... the table with the fish. Then the dog, Rosie, came (10) .... the house and chased the cat. They both ran (11) .... the bushes and (12) .... the patio. Felix stopped suddenly but Rosie fell (13) .... the pond. Felix looked at her and then jumped (14) .... the wall again, still holding the fish.

prepositions (general)

173 Read sentence (a) and then write sentence (b). Use the word in brackets ( ) + a preposition (**to/at/with** etc.).

1 a) I always got the best mark in History at school.
   b) I _was good at History at school._ (good)

2 a) The apples you bought yesterday were green. These are red.
   b) These apples _are different from the ones._ (different)

3 a) Turn the TV off, please. It's football and I don't like it.
   b) I _am not interested in football._ (not interested)

4 a) This is Kate's husband, Carl.
   b) Kate _is married to Carl_ (married)

5 a) Rain, rain, rain! I'd like some sunshine for a change.
   b) I .... (fed up)

6 a) Jim doesn't like storms. They frighten him.
   b) Jim .... (afraid)

7 a) Stuart can't cook. A boiled egg is too difficult for him!
   b) Stuart .... (not very good)

8 a) Oliver always does the shopping for his elderly neighbours.
   b) Oliver .... (nice)

9 a) You can't move in my grandmother's sitting room. She's got a lot of furniture.
   b) My grandmother's sitting room .... (full)

10 a) Why are you shouting at Liz?
   b) Why ....? (angry)

174 Put in a preposition (**of/to/for** etc.) where necessary.

1 It was really nice _of_ Lisa to send you a birthday present. You must write _to_ her and thank her _for_ it.

2 If you've got a problem, you can always talk _to_ Janet _about_ it. She's very good _at_ listening _to_ people.

3 A: What's happened _to_ you? You look very wet.
   B: I was fed up _with_ waiting _for_ a bus so I walked home, but then it started raining.

4 I must remember to telephone _to_ Sarah tonight. I want to ask her _for_ some information about hotels in Madrid. I'm thinking _of_ going there in the autumn.

5 A: Have you got any books ~~from~~ Luke Allen? Do you think I'll like his writing?
   B: It depends _on_ what kind of stories you like. This one, for example, is .... his time in prison.

6 We're going .... holiday on Saturday. Could you look .... the cat for us?

7 A: Martha spent two hours .... the phone last night, talking .... her boyfriend.
   B: What were they talking ....?
   A: I don't know, but she was very nice .... him.

8 A: Does this pen belong .... anyone here?
   B: Yes, me. I've been looking .... it for ages.

9 We didn't have to wait .... the train. It arrived .... time.

175 Complete the sentences. Use a preposition + the verb in brackets ( ).

> *Dear Lynn*
>
> *Thank you* (1) *for sending* *(send) me the photos of John. I'm*
> *sorry* (2) .... *(not / write) before but I've been very busy. My job*
> *is taking a lot of my time at the moment. In fact, I'm thinking*
> (3) .... *(leave). I'm not really interested* (4) .... *(sell)*
> *cars any more. I liked the job at first but now I'm fed up* (5) ....
> *(say) the same things to everyone – you know, how wonderful the cars*
> *are, etc. Do you think I should look for a new job? It's a big decision to*
> *take. I'm a bit afraid* (6) .... *(be) unemployed. I know I'm*
> *good* (7) .... *(sell) things but the employment situation is*
> *difficult at the moment. What's your advice?*
>
> *Hope to hear from you soon.*
> *Love Mark*

go in, put on etc. (phrasal verbs)

Units 107–108 + Appendices 5 and 6

176 Complete the sentences with you **up/off/in** etc.

1 Hurry ..*up*.., Pam! The plane takes ..*off*.. in ten minutes.
2 Jane was asleep on the bus. Suddenly, the bus driver said, 'Wake ....! This is your stop.'
   Jane quickly got .... and the bus drove ....
3 A young boy ran out of the sweet shop and rode .... on his bike. Two seconds later, the
   shop keeper came out and shouted, 'Come ....! You haven't paid!'
4 Look ....! There's an old woman trying to cross the road. I think you're driving too fast.
   Slow .... a bit, please.
5 If you've finished Exercise 6, turn .... and carry .... Exercises 7 and 8 are on page 5.
6 A: Can I speak to Bob, please?
   B: I'm sorry, I can't hear you. Can you speak ....?
   A: Can I speak to Bob, please?
   B: Yes, hold .... a minute. He's in the kitchen, washing .... I'll call him. BOB!
7 One cold night last winter my car broke .... I went to a house and asked for help. The
   man there was very kind and said, 'Come .... and keep warm.'

177 Complete the sentences with a verb + **on/off/up** etc.

1 You're in a clothes shop. You want to buy some jeans but first you want to see if they're the
   right size. What do you ask the shop assistant?
   Can I try these jeans on, please?
2 It's dark in the room. You need some light. What do you ask?
   Could you ...., please?

3 Your father can't read the newspaper because he isn't wearing his glasses.
   What do you tell him to do?
   ...., Dad.

4 You borrow some money from a friend. You promise to return it tomorrow.
   What do you say?
   I'll .... tomorrow.

5 Your grandmother has dropped a magazine on the floor and she can't get it.
   What does she ask you?
   Could you .... for me, please?

6 Your sister is playing her stereo very loudly. You don't mind, but you don't want it so loud.
   What do you ask her?
   Could you .... a bit, please?

7 You are in the sitting room and the TV is on. Your mother comes in and asks if you are
   watching it. What do you say?
   No, not really. You can ....

8 You've found some very old and very soft tomatoes in the fridge. What do you ask?
   Do you want these tomatoes or shall I ....?

when and **if**   Units 110–112

178 Complete the sentences in your own words.

1 Please don't talk to me when I'm *trying to work.*
2 When John finishes university, he ....
3 My grandfather started work at the age of 14 and stopped when he ....
4 Sarah will probably buy a car when she ....
5 When you ...., you'll be surprised how much he's changed.
6 I'll give Stephanie your letter when ....
7 When I first heard the news, ...
8 I'm a bit shy when ....

179 Jill and Sue are waiting at the bus-stop. They are on their way to the cinema. Complete their story.
Use the end of the previous sentence to make the beginning of the next sentence.

Oh dear, the bus is late.
1 If the bus *doesn't arrive* soon, we'll be late.
2 If .... late, we'll miss the beginning of the film.
3 If .... the film, we won't
   understand the story.
4 If .... the story, we'll be bored.
5 If ...., we'll probably fall asleep.
6 If ...., we'll miss the end of the film.
   Let's not go to the cinema.

180 Look at the two underlined parts of these sentences. One part is right and the other is wrong. Correct the wrong part.

1 When <u>you come</u> home tonight, <u>we go</u> and see Fred in hospital.   *.... we will go ....*
2 <u>I'm going to</u> visit the Colosseum when <u>I'll be</u> in Rome. ....
3 <u>Do you tell</u> me what happened when <u>I see</u> you later? ....
4 It's a pity this room is so small. If <u>it were</u> bigger, we <u>can put</u> all our furniture in it. ....
5 If <u>I will see</u> Ann, <u>I won't ask</u> her about her exam. ....
6 Sam doesn't get up early enough to catch the 7.30 train. If <u>he would get up</u> earlier, <u>he wouldn't be</u> late. ....
7 I'm sure Bill <u>will ring</u> you before <u>he will go</u> on holiday. ....
8 If <u>it won't rain</u> soon, all the plants <u>will die</u> in the garden. ....
9 I haven't got a bike, I'm afraid. If <u>I have</u> one, <u>I would lend</u> it to you. ....
10 Barbara is in bed with a fever. <u>She would be</u> here with us if <u>she wouldn't be</u> ill. ....

181 What do you say in the following situations? Use the words in brackets ( ) to help you.

1 Paul has asked you to go to a jazz concert. You don't like jazz so you're not going with him.
(I / go / with you / if I / like / jazz)   *I would go with you if I liked jazz.*

2 You haven't decided what to do this weekend. Perhaps you will go to London or perhaps you will stay at home and invite your boss for dinner.
(If I / not / go / to London / I / invite / my boss for dinner)
If I don't go to London, I'll invite my boss for dinner.

3 You want to go on holiday but you're very busy at work at the moment.
(If I / not / be / busy at work / I / go / on holiday)

4 You're in a restaurant with your sister. She's got some onions on her plate. You know she doesn't like them but you do!
(I / eat your onions / if you / not / want them)

5 You want to buy a new computer. The one you are looking at is quite cheap but it doesn't have a very big memory.
(If it / have / a bigger memory / I / buy / it)

6 You and Clare are outside the cinema, waiting for David. He's late and the film starts in five minutes.
(We / miss the beginning / if he / not / arrive / soon)

7 Your brother is going to buy an old car in bad condition. You don't think it's a good idea.
(I / not / buy it / if I / be / you)

8 I don't have any money because I don't have a job.
(If I / have / a job / I / have / some money)

the person who ... / the people we met
(relative clauses)

Units 113–114

182 Make one sentence from two sentences. Use **who** or **which**.

1 James lives on an island. It's famous for its beautiful beaches.
James _lives on an island which is famous for its beautiful beaches._

2 There's a new chef in our canteen. He's very good at making desserts.
There's a new chef ....

3 A car crashed into mine. It was green.
The car ....

4 Where's the newspaper? It was on the table.
Where .... ?

5 A handbag was left on the bus yesterday. It belongs to my sister.
The handbag .... my sister.

6 I spoke to an assistant. She had long, dark hair.
I ....

7 Peter writes books. They are translated into many languages.
Peter ....

8 A lot of people went to last night's concert. They enjoyed it.
The people ....

183 Make one sentence from two sentences.

1 Jill is looking at a man. She thinks she knows him.
Jill thinks she knows _the man she's looking at._

2 Sally stayed with some friends. What's their name?
What's the name .... ?

3 I worked in a shop. It was called 'Bangles'.
The shop I ....

4 I was talking to some people. They're friends of your father's.
The people I ....

5 You were looking for a woman. Did you find her?
Did you find the .... ?

6 Kate went on holiday with some people. They lived in the same street.
The people ....

7 I'm listening to some music. It was written over 300 years ago.
The music ....

8 Fiona's playing tennis with a man. Who is he?
Who's the .... ?

184 Complete the sentences. Use the information in brackets.

GUIDE: Ladies and gentlemen, this is the house (1) _Michael Barnes was born in._
        (*Michael Barnes was born in this house.*)

CLARE: Who's Michael Barnes?

ADAM: He's the man (2) ....
        (*Michael Barnes wrote over 100 books.*)

CLARE: I've never heard of him.

ADAM: You have! You know that film (3) ....?
        (*We went to see a film last week.*) Well it was based on one of his books.

CLARE: Oh.

GUIDE: And now, if you look on your right you can see Jane Carter's house.

CLARE: Why is that important?

ADAM: You must remember! Jane Carter is the woman (4) ....
        (*I told you about Jane Carter.*)

CLARE: Oh yes. She lived until she was over a hundred.

ADAM: That's right. And do you remember the name of the institute (5) ....
        .... (*The institute was founded by Jane Carter.*)

CLARE: The Fellcome Institute, wasn't it?

ADAM: Yes, and if you remember, it was the Fellcome Institute (6) ....
        ....

        (*The Fellcome Institute was closed down by the authorities in the 1950s.*)

CLARE: I remember now. So this is her house. Interesting.

GUIDE: And now, let's go into the main street and look at …

Key

In many of these answers you can use the full form of the verb (I am, he has, etc.) or the short form of the verb (I'm, she's, etc.).

1

3 are
4 am not (I'm not)
5 is not (isn't)
6 am (*not* I'm – see Unit 39)
7 Are … is … isn't
  or Are … isn't … is
8 is
9 are not (aren't)
10 are ('re)
11 Is
12 are

2

2 What's / What is … ?
3 How's / How is … ?
4 Where are … ?
5 How old is … ?
6 What colour are … ?
7 Why's / Why is … ?
8 Where's / Where is … ?
9 How much are … ?
10 Who's / Who is … ?
11 Why are … ?

3

2 … are very high mountains.
3 … isn't the capital of the USA.
4 … is a popular sport in Britain.
5 Paul is 21 years old today.
6 Britain isn't a hot country.
7 All the shops are closed at lunchtime.
8 I'm not at work this week. I'm on holiday.
9 Too many chocolates aren't good for you.
10 Sally's teacher isn't British. She's American.

4

2 How old is he?
3 Is … your … ?
4 Who's that?
5 How old is she?
6 Is that … ?
7 What's his name?
8 Are … your … ?

5

Example answers (There are a lot more than ten possible sentences in this exercise.)
3 Are your parents old?
4 I am an engineer.

5 How old is Anna?
6 Jim's book isn't expensive.
7 Where is Anna?
8 Your parents aren't at work.
9 How are your parents?
10 I'm not 18.

6

+ ing	t → tt, p → pp etc.
listening	swimming
playing	forgetting
starting	beginning
working	stopping
laughing	winning
wearing	digging
crying	robbing

e → ing	ie → ying
having	lying
writing	tying
arriving	
coming	
living	
dancing	
making	

7

2 writing / is writing / she is writing
3 is making
4 is singing
5 are drinking / are having
6 is talking
7 isn't listening
8 is thinking
9 aren't working
10 are having
11 is ringing
12 isn't sitting
13 is standing
14 is asking

8

2 … aren't playing with a ball. They're playing with a train.
3 Eric isn't wearing sunglasses. He's wearing a hat.
4 Pam isn't cooking chicken. She's cooking fish.
5 She isn't laughing. She's crying.
6 Jo isn't standing with her mother. She's lying on the grass.
7 She isn't eating an orange. She's eating a banana.
8 Fred, the dog, isn't lying on the grass asleep. He's playing with a ball.

9

2 Are they … ?
3 What's (Simon) doing?
4 What's he watching?
5 Is (Anna) watching the programme? *or* … watching TV?
6 What are you doing?

10

2	don't	6	don't
3	have	7	has
4	works	8	speak
5	doesn't	9	don't

11

2 lives … drinks … cries … doesn't read
3 shines … live … falls … doesn't rain
4 have … eat … fly … don't like

12

2 Do you go to the office every day?
3 My car doesn't work when it is cold.
4 What time does the film start?
5 Ben's sister doesn't speak French but Ben does.
6 How many eggs do you want for breakfast?
7 *right*
8 What does your father do?
9 I don't write many letters. I usually use the telephone.
10 What does Sue usually have for lunch?
11 *right*
12 Charlie plays basketball but he doesn't enjoy it.

13

2 St John's Hospital
3 10 p.m.
4 6 o'clock
5 bus
6 taxi
7 20 children
8 many times
9 wakes the children up
10 gives them breakfast
11 very tired

13 do you work?
14 do you start work?
15 do you finish?
16 do you go to work?
17 do you come home (in the morning)?

18 children do you have in your section?
19 do you look at the children?
20 does the day nurse arrive?
21 does she do …
22 do you usually feel …

14

2 Do you go … ?
3 How do you get/travel … ?
4 How much does it cost?
5 Where do you (usually) sit?
6 What/Which kind of films do you like?
7 What's your favourite film?
8 Do you eat/buy … ?

10 walks
11 lives
12 costs
13 sits
14 likes
15 is
16 doesn't eat
17 has/buys/drinks

Example answer
I often go to the cinema with friends. I don't live near the cinema so I usually go by bus. It costs … and I sit in the middle of the cinema. I like all kinds of films, especially science fiction films and my favourite is 'ET'. I often eat popcorn in the cinema and drink coke.

15

2 I don't understand
3 aren't watching
4 is washing
5 are we running
6 is Tom doing
7 does John get up
8 don't go
9 Do you come
10 I always stay
11 Does it snow
12 isn't cooking … (She)'s talking

16

Example answer
a) Every day I get up at 7.30 a.m. and clean my teeth. I listen to music on the radio. And I have a shower.
b) At the moment, I'm sitting in my room and I'm writing this exercise. I'm wearing jeans and a white shirt. And I'm thinking about my lunch.

17

3 does Pam do
4 isn't working
5 are you smiling
6 don't eat meat
7 are you reading
8 do you get up
9 's making coffee

10 do you go to work
11 aren't watching it
12 're learning Greek

18

2 … do you do?
   What are you doing?
3 When do you usually finish work?
   Why are you leaving now?
4 What is John doing?
   Does he watch TV a lot?
5 What are Phillip and Laura doing?
   How much does it cost?
6 Why are they running?
   What time does school start?
   or What time do they start school?

19

(Example answers)
2 Do you read a newspaper every day? *(Yes, I do.)*
3 Does it snow much in your country?
   (No, it doesn't.)
4 Do you usually do your homework on a word processor?
   (No, I don't.)
5 Are you drinking coffee now?
   (Yes, I am.)
6 Do you drink coffee for breakfast every day?
   (No, I don't.)
7 Are you working at the moment?
   (Yes, I am.)
8 Do children eat lunch at school in your country?
   (No, they don't.)

20

2 has got		7 hasn't got	
3 hasn't got		8 has got	
4 have got		9 has got	
5 has got		10 has got	
6 has got		11 haven't got	

21

2 have you got
3 Has she got
4 has it got
5 Has he got
6 Have they got
7 (cats) have they got
8 have you got

22

2 Have you got
3 hasn't got
4 has got
5 haven't got
6 have got
7 has … got

23

2 He was
3 It was
4 They were
5 It was
6 We were
7 They were
8 I was

24

Example answer
2 I was in the city centre
3 I was at the cinema
4 I was at the sports centre
5 I was in bed
6 I was in a restaurant
7 I was in the garden

25

2 Was it difficult … it wasn't.
3 Was it fast? … it was.
4 Were they expensive? … they weren't.
5 Were you lazy? … I wasn't.
6 Was she ill? … she was.
7 Were they famous? … they were.

26

2 didn't open … opened
3 didn't break … broke
4 didn't go … went
5 didn't have … had
6 didn't wear … wore

7 didn't snow
8 didn't watch TV
9 didn't write
10 didn't catch a bus / take a bus *or* didn't go by bus / travel by bus.

27

2 Did you play volleyball?
3 Did you have a big lunch?
4 Did you visit your grandmother?
5 Did you have a history lesson?
6 Did you watch your favourite TV programme?
7 Did you do your homework?
8 Did you spend any money?

28

2 bus
3 half an hour later
4 9.00 a.m.
5 1.00 p.m.
6 an Italian restaurant
7 my brother
8 spaghetti
9 a birthday present
10 the sports centre
11 did some work

13 did you go to college
14 did you arrive (there)
15 did your lessons begin/start
16 did your lessons finish
17 did you go for lunch
18 did you meet there *or* did you have lunch with
19 did you eat/have
20 did you buy after lunch
21 did your brother go
22 did you do in the evening

29

2 Did you have
3 didn't have
4 had
5 Did … have
6 had
7 did they have

30

2 spent/had
3 was
4 visited/saw
5 went/climbed
6 was
7 were
8 took/caught
9 walked/went
10 weren't
11 went
12 enjoyed/liked
13 was

(*Follow the ideas on the postcard for your answer.*)

31

Example answers

2 Yes, very good. I went to the cinema.
3 Yes, it was
4 I went to an Italian restaurant.
5 Wonderful, … I ate *or* it cost
6 I had an accident
7 had
8 repaired it

32

2 Phillip was sitting in the garden.
3 Rosa was working in her room, *or* … in the house.
4 Paul was repairing his car.
5 Sam's dogs were playing in the park.
6 Mrs Drake was going into the baker's.
7 Sam was climbing a tree in the park.
8 Lynn was lying on the grass in the park.
9 Mike and Tim were waiting at the bus-stop.

Example answers

10 At 10.30 a.m. yesterday I was sitting in my office.
11 At 12.30 p.m. I was having lunch.
12 At 4.00 p.m. I was writing a letter.
13 At 8.30 p.m. I was cooking the dinner.
14 At 1.00 a.m. I was sleeping.

33

1 Did you see … was reading
2 telephoned … was sitting … drinking … Was … was working … did you go … went
3 broke … was washing … were … dropped
4 Did you think … was … didn't write … was dreaming

5 was … happened … was raining … weren't going … broke … cut
6 wasn't talking … were you talking

34

2 Where was Joan Turner?
3 What was Mrs Jones doing?
4 Where was Mrs Walters going?
5 How many robbers went into the bank?
6 Were they carrying guns?
7 Where was the big car waiting?
8 Was the driver a man or a woman?
9 Did you see a man in an old jacket on the corner?
10 Were some men repairing the road?
11 Was anyone waiting at the bus-stop?
13 was in the baker's.
14 was walking along the street.
15 was going into the baker's.
16 Three … went into
17 were carrying
18 was waiting opposite (*or* in front of) the bank
19 was a woman
20 was standing on the corner
21 were repairing
22 were waiting

35

3 What does he do?
4 What does he study?
5 What does he like?
6 Where did he go for his last holiday? or … did he spend his last … ?
7 Where did he stay?
8 What did he do on holiday?

Example answer

9 Jill is 29 and she comes from Dublin. She's a computer programmer and she studied mathematics at university. She likes travelling, swimming and chocolate. Last month she went to Indonesia for one month. She went camping and she did lots of walking.

(*Follow Jill's paragraph for your answer.*)

36

6 Did (you) see
7 I (never) watch
8 was
9 showed
10 are (you) looking
11 are wearing

12 bought
13 is (Jim) doing
14 happened
15 fell
16 hurt
17 was running
18 Was (Sally) working
19 was helping
20 helps
21 did (she) go
22 stayed

37

2 was
3 went
4 was sitting
5 visited
6 saw
7 was
8 was
9 is
10 made
11 was
12 was
13 had
14 did it happen
15 were both riding
16 stopped
17 fell
18 broke
19 talk
20 Do you ride
21 stopped
22 moved
23 do you do
24 like
25 swim
26 love
27 am making
28 is swimming

38

3 it has disappeared
4 I've already seen … have you seen
5 I haven't finished it
6 they've gone out
7 Has he lost
8 I haven't heard from her
9 you've broken it
10 have you been
11 have you taken
12 I haven't heard

39

2 've already told her
3 haven't read it yet
4 hasn't had it yet
5 's already written
6 hasn't driven it yet
7 've already sold it

40

2 Have you ever had … Have you ever broken
3 Have you ever travelled
4 Have you ever flown
5 Have you ever lost
6 Have you ever slept
7 Have you ever climbed

Two of the following:
Jack has broken his leg twice.
Jack has travelled in a canoe.
Jack has flown in a helicopter.
Jack has slept outside.
Jack has climbed a high mountain.

Two of the following:
Jack has never had a serious illness.
Jack has never eaten crocodile.
Jack has never lost his way.

Example answers
I've never ridden a camel.
I've broken my arm once. *etc.*

41

2 have ... gone
  have ... been
3 have(n't) been
4 has gone
5 has gone ... has ... been

42

2 have done
3 has travelled/been
4 has met/seen
5 has made/earned
6 has ... written
7 has ridden
8 has ... sold/sent
9 have played
10 have ... been

43

2 How long have you been
3 How long has she worked
4 How long have you had
5 How long have they known
6 How long has he been

44

1 Tony has worked here since ...
  his birthday
  he left school
  this morning
  2 o'clock yesterday
  the beginning of April
  Christmas
  1992
2 John has been married for ...
  more than 2 years
  a long time
  6 weeks
  4 months

45

Example answers
3 six months ago
4 for six months
5 two years ago
6 for two days
7 ten years ago ... 3 years ago
8 for a few weeks

46

2 've been waiting for Sam since 7.00 p.m.
3 've been walking for six hours.
4 've been watching TV since 9 o'clock this morning.
5 's been raining since last week.

6 has been feeling sick since lunchtime.
7 've been building our house for six months.
8 has been travelling since June 28th. *or* has been travelling for 4 days.

47

2 When did John lose his job?
3 When was the last time you had a holiday?
4 How long has Jill had a cat?
5 What time did you finish work?
6 How long did you watch TV last night?
7 When did Chris go out?
8 How long has your father been in hospital?

48

3 Brasilia has been the capital of Brazil since 1960. Before 1960, Rio de Janeiro was the capital.
4 Carol moved to Oxford in 1975. She has lived / has been living in Oxford since 1975.
5 I haven't seen the new manager yet. When did she start working for the company?
6 You spoke good French on the telephone yesterday. How long have you learned / have you been learning it?
7 Paula and Laurence have been married since last year. They met at university.
8 Peter has never tried Japanese food. He went to Japan last year but he ate hamburgers.
9 I broke my arm six months ago. I've used / have been using a computer for my work since then.
10 My brother has been a professional footballer since 1994. But when he was younger he didn't like sport very much.

49

3 reached
4 have started
5 did (they) spend
6 took
7 has changed
8 won
9 has/have won
10 was
11 scored
12 has been
13 left
14 arrived
15 has been

16 said
17 have worked / have been working
18 has been
19 have had / have been having
20 was

50

2 have lost ... did ... see ... left
3 bought ... has ... had
4 haven't finished ... started
5 Did ... see ... Have ... seen ... have touched ... was ... was
6 failed ... has she failed

51

2 was
3 did you do
4 was hanging
5 hit
6 have you been waiting
7 is hurting

9 is driving
10 telephoned
11 asked
12 've never been late
13 did my mother forget

15 have you been working
16 Do you like
17 was
18 Have you ... had
19 did it happen
20 Was it
21 are you driving/going
22 are you looking
23 is
24 Has it gone/disappeared

52

2 was
3 watched
4 ate
5 had
6 enjoyed
7 'm writing
8 'm sitting
9 had
10 was
11 've been
12 came
13 have / have got
14 was
15 Do you like
16 is
17 's practising
18 've just sent
19 did you find / have you found
20 left
21 's sitting

22 Thank you for your letter. Yes, I enjoyed the time you spent with me very much. We had some good fun!

23 You left a wonderful box of chocolates for my parents. Thank you. We've just finished them – they were delicious.
24 And thank you also for the cassettes. They arrived yesterday. I haven't played all of them yet. At the moment I'm listening to one. 'Paradise Rock'. It's very good.
25 My mother found your photo album the day you left. I sent it back two weeks ago. Have you received it yet?
26 Do you remember Steve? We met him at Sue's party. Well, he came to my house last week. He asked for your address so I gave it to him. I hope that's OK. He's in California now on business.
27 I'm looking out of the window at the moment. The sun's shining and it's a beautiful, warm day. In fact, it's been sunny every day since you went back to San Francisco. Sorry!
28 The cassette has just finished. Tell your brother I love his music. Does he want a publicity agent in London?

(Use Dear Jo letter as an example.)

53
2 were … developed
3 Was … invented
4 were … made
5 were … produced
6 was … built

54
3 is locked
4 are checked
5 is being made
6 are being put
7 isn't exported
8 is washed
9 is allowed
10 is being served

55
3 The window has been closed.
4 The computer has been turned off.
5 The chair has been repaired.
6 The cups haven't been washed.
7 The lights haven't been turned off.

56
3 was taken
4 caused
5 were covered

6 left
7 walked
8 are being removed
9 are being repaired
10 is (now) moving

11 was stolen
12 telephoned
13 was seen
14 drove
15 are looking

16 have (just) heard
17 blew
18 is waiting
19 was
20 was sent off
21 kicked

22 was hurt
23 crashed
24 was taken
25 played / were playing
26 is being taken
27 thinks
28 is happening
29 are walking

57
2 has   7 were
3 was   8 weren't
4 doesn't 9 are
5 haven't 10 didn't
6 is

58
2 Do I   6 did you
3 Are you   7 was it
4 do they   8 Has she
5 Have you 9 Were you

59
3 gave … forgot
4 found … left
5 showed … taken
6 escaped … caught
7 thought … done
8 wore … given
9 learned/learnt … fell … swum
10 felt … went … slept
11 hit … hurt … forgotten

60
2 used to be
3 used to play
4 used to swim/fish
5 used to live
6 used to walk
7 used to eat/cook
8 used to be
9 used to be

Example answer
I used to play the piano. *etc.*

61
2 used to live
3 used to hunt
4 wear
5 used to cook
6 used to take off
7 used to spend
8 used to wear/have
9 drive/have
10 used to take
11 used to go
12 have
13 used to be
14 hate

62
2 'm having   6 'm driving
3 is coming   7 does … start
4 is getting   8 'm talking
5 are going   9 leaves

Example answers
11 I'm going to the cinema.
12 I'm having lunch with my sister.
13 I'm playing football.
14 I'm working on Sunday.

63
3 The next bus leaves in five minutes.
4 Where are you going at the weekend?
5 It doesn't finish late.
6 Jane is working at Brown's Restaurant tonight so she can't come to the party.
7 He's leaving for France at 5 o'clock tomorrow.
8 Where does the next train go to? *or* Where is the next train going to?

64
2 What are you going to buy for Paul's birthday? … Is he going to have a party?
3 Are you going to buy a new computer? … What kind are you going to get?
4 What is Sarah going to do after university? … How long is she going to be away?
5 Are Joe and Kate going to get married? … Where are they going to live?

65
2 He's going to have / There's going to be
3 She's going to be
4 He's going to
5 They're going to
6 I'm going to

66

3 No, he won't. He'll probably be in the city centre.
4 True.
5 No, he won't. He'll be with his friends.
6 True.
7 No, he won't. He'll be 31.
8 No, they won't. They'll probably be at school.
9 He doesn't know where he'll be in 2020.

Example answers
This evening I'll probably be at home.
Tomorrow morning I'll be at school/work. *etc.*

67

2 'll stay   4 won't see
3 won't tell   5 'll get

68

2 Shall I make/get
3 Shall I close
4 Shall I do/open
5 Shall I turn
6 Shall I take
7 Shall I clean/wash

69

2 Shall we stay
3 Shall we use/take
4 Shall we drive *or* go by car …
5 shall we go
6 Shall we ask/invite

70

2 is having … goes
3 doesn't often stay … is staying
4 Are you taking … Do you want
5 am cooking … does

71

2 I'll buy you another one.
3 I'm going shopping with my sister.
4 I'll telephone you this evening.
5 Tony and Rachel are coming to dinner tonight.
6 I don't think you'll like it.
7 What are you doing at the weekend?
8 I'm staying at home all weekend.

72

3 'm going   8 'll rain
4 'll make   9 *right*
5 does … rise   10 'll call
6 are you going   11 *right*
7 *right*

73

2 When does the next term begin?
   What are you going to do during …
   I don't finish until … Then, I'm going to look for a job …
3 I'm going to visit …
   I'm going to take it to …
   I'll lend you mine.
   I'll buy the petrol.
4 Is everybody coming to the meeting?
   Do you think it'll be a long … ?
   It'll probably be about …
   I'm going to the dentist …

74

2 might take/get a taxi … they might not come.
3 I might invite/ask Sarah …
   I might not invite/ask Tony.
4 She might buy some jeans … she might not buy anything.

Example answers
6 I might play tennis.
7 I might go shopping.
8 I might not go to Maria's party.

75

3 He's going to walk along The Great Wall.
4 He might try the rice wine.
5 He's not going to eat western food.
6 He might go on a boat trip.
7 He's going to learn a few phrases of Chinese.
8 He might not come home.

76

2 can see
3 can't get in
4 can't climb
5 can't telephone
6 can hear

8 could see
9 couldn't get in
10 couldn't climb
11 couldn't telephone
12 could hear

77

3 can't type
4 couldn't understand
5 couldn't answer
6 can't come
7 couldn't catch
8 can't speak
9 can't see

78

3 Can/Could you give me a wake-up call at 6.30 in the morning, please?
4 Can/Could I have breakfast in my room tomorrow morning, please?
5 Can/Could I leave my passport and travellers cheques in the hotel safe, please?
6 Can/Could I borrow a hair dryer, please?
7 Can/Could you get a taxi for me, please?

79

2 had to work
3 must bring/get/have
4 mustn't eat/have
5 had to go
6 mustn't be
7 must wash
8 had to climb

80

3 mustn't ask
4 needn't read
5 needn't ask
6 mustn't work
7 mustn't leave
8 mustn't read
9 needn't leave
10 needn't work

81

2 You should go
   You shouldn't eat/have
3 You should take/have
   You shouldn't work/read
4 You should take/have/get
   You shouldn't smoke/have
5 You should tell
   You shouldn't lend/give

82

2 Do you think I should ask
3 Do you think I/we should wait
4 Do you think I/we should wake
5 Do you think I/we should go
6 Do you think we should take/ catch/get
7 Do you think I/we should buy/ get/have

83

Example answers
2 she should go out more
3 they should go out every night
4 he should do what he wants
5 you should tell her

84

2 Does he have to get up
3 did you have to take
4 do you have to finish/read

5 Did she have to go
6 do you have to be

85

2 Do I have to write
3 doesn't have to go
4 don't have to shout
5 had to work
6 doesn't have to decide
7 Did you have to walk
8 has to stay
9 didn't have to tell

86

1 it … there
2 there … there … it
3 it … there
4 there … there … There … it … It

87

2 There are
3 there were
4 there was
5 there is
6 there will be
7 there is
8 There has been

88

2 It's
3 there wasn't
4 it was
5 There's
6 it was
7 it was
8 there was
9 it's
10 It isn't

12 Is it raining at the moment?
13 Is it sunny at the moment?
14 Is there any snow in winter?
15 Was there any snow last winter?

89

3 Simon lives in a town but David doesn't.
4 Simon isn't married but David is.
5 Simon has got brothers and sisters but David hasn't.
6 Simon was good at school but David wasn't.
7 Simon didn't study at university but David did.
8 Simon's going on holiday this year but David isn't.
9 Simon hasn't visited many countries but David has.

90

2 Don't you?
3 Can't he?
4 Has she?
5 Did I?
6 Doesn't he?
7 Hasn't it?
8 Aren't you?
9 Were you?
10 Was it?

91

2 didn't you
3 do you
4 haven't you
5 isn't it
6 were they
7 have you

92

3 … is too.
4 I haven't either.
5 I don't either.
6 I did too.
7 I am too.
8 Mine isn't either.

93

3 Neither can Mary.
4 Neither is Mary.
5 Mary does.
6 Neither has Mary.
7 Mary isn't.
8 So did Mary.
9 Neither does Mary.
10 So will Mary.

Example answers
John isn't married and neither am I.
Mary went to university and so did I. *etc.*

94

2 haven't had
3 doesn't do
4 don't watch … don't like
5 'm not reading
6 didn't come
7 don't look
8 isn't raining
9 hasn't eaten

95

2 wasn't born
3 didn't live
4 can't speak
5 haven't got / don't have
6 isn't
7 don't live
8 won't be
9 'm not going to buy
10 don't want / wouldn't like

96

2 What do you do?
3 Did you go to university? / Did you study at university?
4 Are you married?
5 Where did you meet your wife?
6 Have you got / Do you have any children?
7 Does Emily go to school?
8 Does your wife work?
9 Do you enjoy your job?
10 Is it a difficult job?
11 How many weeks holiday do you have/get?

97

3 did you buy
4 wants
5 are you going to say / will you say

6 likes
7 's playing
8 happened
9 does it mean

98

2 's he waiting for
3 did you write to
4 does he come from
5 does she live/share with
6 's it about
7 's it famous for
8 did you sell it to
9 's she looking at

99

3 How far did you
4 What colour is
5 How tall is
6 Which shoes shall I

100

2 Why didn't you ring me last night?
3 Who are you giving that present to?
4 How much has Mary spent?
5 Where did Jenny go for her holidays last year?
6 What do you usually do in the evenings?
7 What happened next?
8 When was the Taj Mahal built?

101

1 did you go … did you go with / went with you … was the weather like?
2 's happened / happened / have you done … did you do that … Does it
3 do you do … Do you work/ teach … do you teach … have you been a teacher / have you been teaching

102

2 I don't know why she's leaving.
3 I don't know when they are getting married.
4 I don't know how much it cost.
5 I don't know who told me.
6 I don't know what he bought me!

103

2 Do you know why all the shops are closed today?
3 Do you know where the Regent Hotel is?
4 Do you know why John is going to leave his job?
5 Do you know when Mrs Smith died?

104

2 Do you know what he was wearing?
3 Do you know who was with him? *or* who he was with?
4 Do you know how much it / the camera cost?
5 Do you know what (kind of) shop he went into?
6 Do you know why the person (with him) was laughing?
7 Do you know where the train was going to?
8 Do you know how long the journey usually takes?

105

3 he had (got) a few days holiday
4 (he) was going to Italy
5 he was ill
6 (he) had been in bed for two days
7 she didn't like parties
8 (she) couldn't dance
9 she loved parties
10 (she) would be free on Saturday

106

2 said   6 told
3 told   7 say
4 said   8 tell
5 said

107

2 you didn't work here on Mondays.
3 you had gone out.
4 Simon said you were at lunch and (you) would be back soon.
5 Mike said you left early on Mondays.
6 Diana said you were making a cup of tea.
7 Mary said she didn't know.

108

2 to meet   8 to have
3 stopping   9 to tell
4 go   10 write
5 to leave   11 to be
6 turn   12 to buy
7 looking

109

3 to leave   9 slowing
4 to be   10 to see
5 to tell   11 to come
6 to drive   12 dancing
7 to let   13 to go
8 to do   14 writing

110

2 taught me to drive.
3 told David not to play with those matches.
4 didn't let his young sons play with toy guns.
5 persuaded Jane to come swimming with us.
6 didn't expect you to marry him.
7 made me pay back all the money I borrowed. *or* ... had borrowed.

111

Example answers
3 invite her to my party.
4 some information.
5 some fresh air.
6 watch a science programme.
7 to make a cup of coffee. *or* for a knife.
8 for your holiday. *or* to pay the bills.
9 to finish her work. *or* for sport.
10 for a letter. *or* to see the new Disney film.

112

2 wrong   3 wrong
  right   right
  right   wrong

4 right
  right
  wrong

113

3 learning   7 to look for
4 asking   8 answering
5 to speak   9 to wait
6 to meet   10 shopping

114

3 holding   10 finishing
4 having   11 to go
5 to swim   12 do
6 cooking   13 to be
7 to make   14 telling
8 help   15 to live
9 learn

115

2 they're not looking at us.
3 I don't want to talk to her.
4 you don't write to them.
5 he doesn't want to meet me.
6 we can't telephone you.
7 they don't visit him.

116

2 my   7 its
3 our   8 her
4 their   9 his
5 its   10 your
6 His

117

3 your   13 him
4 me   14 him
5 my   15 them
6 mine   16 Their
7 They   17 hers
8 them   18 mine
9 I   19 yours
10 us   20 their
11 his   21 your
12 he

118

4 by herself
5 each other
6 myself
7 each other
9 cut themselves
10 understand each other
11 went by herself
12 enjoyed ourselves
13 wrote ... each other

119

3 James gave me those books. I really like them.
4 Some friends of theirs told them the news.
5 Patty gave her brother a cassette and he gave her a video.
6 My brother and his wife are not happy together. They don't love each other any more.
7 John is a good friend of mine.
8 *right*
9 I like this house but its windows are broken.
10 I know Mary but I don't know her brother.
11 I sometimes ask myself why I work in a noisy, dirty city.

120

2 Ann's car.
3 king's palace.
4 Caroline's garden.
5 Elena's house
6 the students' books
7 my sister's birthday.
8 Mrs Penn's cakes
9 grandparents' house
10 Chris's parents.

121

2 The football shirt is Mike's.
3 The (running) shoes are Alan's.
4 The guitar is Alan's.
5 The chocolates are Mike's. *or* The box of chocolates is Mike's.
6 The computer game is Alan's.
7 The books are Alan's.
8 The magazine is Mike's.

122

3 John's favourite team
4 the end of the programme
5 your parents' anniversary party
6 the windows of the house
7 the telephone number of the station
8 Mr Turner's daughter
9 your aunt's wedding

123

2 an empty glass
3 a difficult question
4 an old book
5 a hot day *or* a warm day
6 a cheap hotel
7 a young man
8 a heavy bag

124

2	knives	7	children
3	tomatoes	8	teeth
4	monkeys	9	women
5	babies	10	sheep

125

2 some information
3 an envelope
4 some perfume
5 a paper
6 some bad news
7 some new socks
8 beautiful weather
9 (some) work
10 a new job
11 some fruit

126

2 some cassettes, a personal stereo, some perfume / a bottle of perfume and a pair of sunglasses.
3 some books, a pair of jeans, some face cream and a map.
4 two pairs of trousers, some T-shirts, some money and a raincoat.

Example answer
I'm going to take a pair of sunglasses, some books, five T-shirts, a camera, *etc.*

127

2 The (first bus)
3 a (musician) ... the (best)
4 an (idea) ... the (new)
5 the (station) ... a (taxi) ... the (city centre)
6 the (kitchen) ... a (guest) ... the (dining room)
7 the (capital) ... a (small city)
8 the (third floor) ... an (old building)

9 a (large town) ... the (middle of) ... the (country) ... a (dog) ... the (dog)
10 a (science fiction movie) ... The (beginning of) the (film) ... the (end)
11 the (same street) ... an (older brother) ... the (most handsome)
12 the (nearest) ... the (end of) ... the (left) ... a (bus-stop)

128

3 the station manager
4 an Italian restaurant
5 on the left
6 the Information Centre
7 the restaurant
8 a woman
9 the kitchen
10 the man
11 *right*
12 exactly the same
13 the papers
14 to the police
15 *right*
16 a knife

129

2 Football
3 history ... the history
4 the photos ... photos
5 The trees ... trees
6 food ... the food
7 The chicken ... chicken
8 hotels
9 the money ... Money

130

2	–	11	the
3	the	12	–
4	the	13	the
5	the	14	the
6	–	15	–
7	–	16	–
8	the	17	–
10	–		

131

2	any	7	some
3	some	8	any
4	some	9	some
5	some	10	any
6	any	11	some

132

2 some milk
3 some information
4 any matches
5 some mistakes
6 some shampoo
7 any chairs/furniture
8 any snow
9 some jam

133

2 anyone/anybody
3 someone/somebody
4 something
5 anyone/anybody
6 something
7 anyone/anybody
8 anything
9 Someone/Somebody
10 anything

134

3 I've got no grandparents.
4 There isn't any time to visit the museums.
5 We had no rain in July last year.
6 There aren't any clouds in the sky today.
7 There wasn't any sugar in my tea.
8 Tim has no books in his house.

135

2	any	6	any
3	*right*	7	*right*
4	*right*	8	no
5	any	9	some

136

2	None	7	some
3	no	8	any
4	any	9	any
5	Some	10	some
6	no		

137

2 anything
3 Nobody/No-one
4 anything
5 anybody/anyone
6 Nothing
7 anything
8 Nobody/No-one
9 Nothing
10 nobody/no-one
11 anybody/anyone

138

2 nowhere
3 nothing
4 somebody/someone
5 somewhere
6 Nobody/No-one
7 someone/somebody
8 anything
9 something
10 anywhere

139

2 nothing to do
3 anyone/anybody to play with
4 anywhere to sit
5 anywhere to stay
6 something to wear
7 anything to say / to talk about

140

2 every ... was
3 Every ... is
4 Every ... has
5 Every ... was

141

2 Every morning
3 all morning
4 every summer
5 all summer
6 all summer
7 Every night
8 all night
9 all night
10 every day
11 all day
12 every day

142

2 Everybody/Everyone is
3 everyone/everybody ... watches
4 everywhere/everything was
5 everything was
6 Everywhere is

143

2	Most of	8	Some
3	Some of	9	None of
4	any	10	no
5	None of	11	any of
6	all	12	all
7	most of		

144

2 Some of Richard's colleagues walk to work. *or* Some of them walk ...
3 All Richard's colleagues have got a car. *or* All of them have ...
4 Most of Richard's colleagues use their car every day. *or* Most of them use ...
5 Some of Lisa's friends go the cinema every month.
6 All Lisa's friends play some kind of sport. *or* All of them play ...
7 None of Lisa's friends study every night. *or* None of them study ...
8 Most of Lisa's friends enjoy dancing. *or* Most of them enjoy ...

145

Example answers
2 Some of it.
3 Most of them.
4 All of them.
5 Some of them.
6 None of it.
7 All of it.

146

3 Either
4 Neither
5 both
6 Both
7 either of
8 both of
9 Neither of
10 either of

147

Example answers
3 Both of us like jazz dance.
4 Neither of us has got a brother.
5 Both of us go jogging every day.
6 Neither of us is married.
7 Both of us have to learn English.
8 Neither of us drives a car.

148

2 There isn't any orange juice.
3 There isn't much cake.
4 There aren't many people.
5 There aren't any sandwiches.
6 There isn't much fish.
7 There aren't many cherries.

149

Example answers
2 How much milk do you like in your coffee? (*Not much.*)
3 How many cars can you see out of the window? (*Not very many.*)
4 How much money do you spend in one month? (*A lot.*)
5 How many good friends do you have? (*A few.*)
6 How much football do you play? (*None.*)
7 How many pairs of socks do you have? (*A lot.*)
8 How much fruit do you eat every day? (*Not much.*)
9 How much water do you drink every day? (*A little.*)

150

2	a few	5	little
3	a few	6	a little
4	little		

151

2 old hotel
3 hot water
4 famous places/sights
5 delicious food/meals
6 friendly people
7 difficult language
8 busy roads/streets/towns
9 big country/place

152

3 happy/pleased
4 hard/heavily
5 smell ... good/wonderful/delicious
6 teacher ... (very) well
7 carefully
8 workers ... hard
9 badly
10 miserable/unhappy/sad/angry

153

2	good	6	well
3	well	7	well
4	good	8	good
5	good		

154

2 City life is not as friendly as village life but it is more exciting.
3 Motorways are not as interesting as country roads but they are faster.
4 Travelling by plane is not as cheap as travelling by bus but it is more comfortable.
5 Egypt is not as green as Iceland but it is warmer.
6 Bicycles are not as comfortable as cars but they are easier to park.

155

2 My computer is <u>more modern</u> than yours.
3 Jack is a <u>better</u> player than me.
4 *right*
5 Is it more interesting <u>than</u> his last book?
6 *right*
7 My mother is the same age <u>as</u> my father.
8 Ann's headache is <u>worse</u> today.
9 She lives much <u>further</u> away now.

156

2	than	8	colder/worse
3	more	9	as
4	as	10	as
5	as	11	more
6	more	12	than
7	more		

(Follow the ideas in the paragraph about the USA and Australia.)

157

4 Life is more expensive than it was.
5 People are not as friendly as they were.
6 Films are more violent than they were.
7 People live longer than they did.

8 Houses are better than they were.
9 Families are not as big as they were.
10 Children have (got) more freedom than they had.
11 People eat better food than they did.

158
2 Who's / Who is the most interesting person you've met?
3 What's / What is the most frightening experience you've had?
4 What's / What is the worst film you've seen?
5 What's / What is the most expensive thing you've bought?
6 What's / What is the most unusual food you've eaten?
7 Which is the largest city you've been to?
8 What's / What is the most useful present you've received?

159
3 enough plates
4 study enough
5 enough people
6 sweet enough
7 enough information
8 fit enough

10 sharp enough to cut
11 enough money to get/buy
12 well enough to go
13 enough time to answer
14 warm enough to sit

160
3 it's too
4 were too many
5 's too
6 had/drank too much
7 it's too
8 it's too

161
3 aren't enough cinemas.
4 's too much noise and dirt.
5 parks are too small. *or* parks aren't big enough.
6 aren't enough things to do after work.
7 are too many tourists.

(Follow the ideas in the exercise to help you.)

162
3 No, they're not old enough to get married. *or* They're too young to …
4 Yes, he's old enough to drive a car.

5 No, she's not old enough to buy a dog. *or* She's too young to …
6 Yes, he's old enough to leave school.
7 No, she's too young to become a Member of Parliament. *or* She's not old enough to …

163
2 I <u>have already won</u> two tennis championships.
3 Maria <u>rarely goes</u> to bed before midnight.
4 *right.*
5 My brother and I <u>still live</u> at home.
6 When do <u>you usually do</u> your homework?
7 I <u>can never remember</u> my car registration number.
8 My sister <u>is sometimes</u> horrible to me.
9 Clare speaks Spanish and she <u>also understands</u> Italian.
10 John and Steve? They <u>are both</u> married now.
11 My younger brother <u>has just finished</u> school.

164
2 has still got it / still has it
3 'm still / still feel
4 still goes
5 still go/swim
6 's still

165
2 'm still looking for my/the keys … haven't found them yet
3 's still raining … haven't seen the sun yet
4 haven't got up yet … 'm still in
5 hasn't apologised yet … 'm still

166
2 at midnight
3 on November 22nd 1963
4 at Christmas
5 at night
6 in winter
7 at 6.30 a.m.
8 in 1900
9 in six weeks
10 on Thursday

167
2 at
3 on
4 since
5 until
6 at
7 in
8 on
9 –
10 in
11 at
12 Until
13 for
14 from … to … at

168
2 to
3 During
4 After
5 while
6 for
7 before
8 since
9 until

169
3 on
4 After
5 in
6 from
7 to
8 until
9 at
10 for
11 At
12 while
13 Before
14 until
15 since
16 In
17 At

(Use the paragraph about Jess to help you.)

170
2 It's on the left, on the top shelf, between the pasta and the bread.
3 They're on the right, on the bottom shelf, opposite the nuts.
4 It's on the right, on the middle shelf, next to the cola.
5 It's on the right, on the top shelf, above the cola.
6 They're below the cola, on the bottom shelf, in the middle, between the biscuits and the chocolate.

Example answers
7 on the right, on the top shelf, opposite the bread.
8 on the left. It's on the middle shelf, in the middle, between the sugar and the eggs.

171
2 at
3 in
4 at
5 to
6 at
7 in
8 at
9 in
10 to
11 to
12 to
13 to
14 –

172
3 past/(a)round
4 along
5 (a)round
6 under
7 on/onto
8 on
9 off
10 out of
11 through
12 across
13 into
14 over

173
2 are different from the ones/ apples you bought yesterday.
3 'm not interested in football.
4 is married to Carl.

5 'm fed up with (the) rain.
6 is afraid of storms.
7 isn't very good at cooking.
8 is nice to his elderly neighbours.
9 is full of furniture.
10 are you angry with Liz.

174

1 ... and thank her <u>for</u> it.
2 ... you can always talk <u>to</u> Janet about it. She's very good <u>at</u> listening <u>to</u> people.
3 What's happened <u>to</u> you? I was fed up <u>with</u> waiting for a bus ...
4 I must remember to telephone Sarah tonight. I want to ask her <u>for</u> some ... I'm thinking <u>of</u>/<u>about</u> going ...
5 Have you got any books <u>by</u> ... It depends (<u>on</u>) what kind of ... This one, for example is <u>about</u> his ...
6 We're going on holiday on Saturday. Could you look <u>after</u> the cat for us?
7 Martha spent two hours <u>on</u> the phone ... She was talking <u>to</u> her ... What were they talking <u>about</u>? ... but she was very nice <u>to</u> him.
8 Does this pen belong <u>to</u> anyone here? Yes, me. I've been looking <u>for</u> it ...
9 We didn't have to wait <u>for</u> the train. It arrived <u>on</u> time.

175

2 about/for not writing
3 of/about leaving
4 in selling
5 with saying
6 of being
7 at selling

176

2 up ... off ... away/off
3 off/away ... back
4 out ... down
5 over ... on
6 up ... on ... up
7 down ... in

177

2 turn/switch the light on or turn /switch on the light
3 Put your glasses on
4 give it / the money back (to you) or give (you) back the money
5 pick it up
6 turn it / your stereo down or turn down your stereo
7 turn it off
8 throw them away

178

Example answers
2 is going to look for a new job.
3 was 65.
4 moves to the country.
5 see Kevin again
6 I see her.
7 I couldn't believe it.
8 I meet new people.

179

2 we're
3 we miss the beginning of
4 we don't understand
5 we're bored
6 we fall asleep

180

2 I'm going to visit the Colosseum when <u>I'm</u> in Rome.
3 <u>Will you tell</u> me what happened when I see you later?
4 If it were bigger, we <u>could put</u> all our furniture in it.
5 If <u>I see</u> Ann, I won't ask her about her exam.
6 If he <u>got up</u> earlier, he wouldn't be late.
7 I'm sure Bill will ring you before <u>he goes</u> on holiday.
8 If <u>it doesn't rain</u> soon, all the plants will die in the garden.
9 If <u>I had</u> one, I would lend it to you.
10 She would be here with us if <u>she wasn't/weren't</u> ill.

181

3 If I weren't/wasn't busy at work, I'd go on holiday.
4 I'll eat your onions if you don't want them.
5 If it had a bigger memory, I would buy it.
6 We're going to miss the beginning if he doesn't come/ arrive soon. or We'll miss ...
7 I wouldn't buy it if I were/was you.
8 If I had a job, I would have some money.

182

2 in our canteen who's very good at making desserts.
3 which crashed into mine was green.
4 's the newspaper which was on the table.
5 which was left on the bus yesterday belongs to my sister.
6 spoke to an assistant who had long, dark hair.
7 writes books which are translated into many languages.
8 who went to last night's concert enjoyed it.

183

2 of the friends Sally stayed with.
3 worked in was called 'Bangles'.
4 was talking to are friends of your father's.
5 woman you were looking for.
6 Kate went on holiday with live in the same street.
7 I'm listening to was written over 300 years ago.
8 man Fiona's playing tennis with?

184

2 who wrote over 100 books.
3 (that/which) we went to see last week.
4 I told you about.
5 which/that was founded by her *or* she founded
6 which/that was closed down by the authorities in the 1950s.